TEENAGE SUICIDE NOTES

THE COSMOPOLITAN LIFE

THE COSMOPOLITAN LIFE

Teenage Suicide Notes: An Ethnography of Self-Harm, Terry Williams

TEENAGE SUICIDE NOTES

AN ETHNOGRAPHY OF SELF-HARM

TERRY WILLIAMS

COLUMBIA UNIVERSITY PRESS

New York

Columbia University Press
Publishers Since 1893
New York   Chichester, West Sussex
cup.columbia.edu

Library of Congress Cataloging-in-Publication Data
Names: Williams, Terry, author.
Title: Teenage suicide notes : an ethnography
of self-harm / Terry Williams.
Description: New York : Columbia University Press, 2017.
Includes bibliographical references and index.
Identifiers: LCCN 2016031347 | ISBN 978-0-231-17790-0 (cloth :
alk. paper) | ISBN 978-0-231-54250-0 (e-book)
Subjects: LCSH: Teenagers—Suicidal behavior—United States. |
Adolescent psychology—United States. | Self-mutilation—United
States. | Self-destructive behavior—United States.
Classification: LCC HV6546 .W555 2017 | DDC 362.280925350973—dc23
LC record available at https://lccn.loc.gov/2016031347
♾
Columbia University Press books are printed on permanent and
durable acid-free paper.
Printed in the United States of America
COVER DESIGN: James Victore

This book is dedicated to Chloe Lee.

CONTENTS

Illustrations can be found on pages 108–117.

PROFILED TEENS

Kyra: a smart, sensitive, and beautiful seventeen-year-old girl struggling to understand her desire to be heroic in death

Enoch: a rural kid involved in self-mutilation and bloodletting rituals with his girlfriend and his friends

Candy: a religious girl from the backwoods of Middle America, who shot herself in a bedroom of her family's home

David: a tall, lanky, middle-class kid with freckles who hung himself in the garage

Tucker: a gay boy from the suburbs who comes out

Gita: a biracial girl struggling to find herself after a rape and descent into strip club life

Boots: a handsome, overachieving jock who talks about queer theory, cross-dresses, and loves Charles Bronson and Clint Eastwood movies

Jill: a West Coast girl who cuts herself to feel alive

Cody: a runaway

Gabriella: a lesbian teenager, taught to hate boys, who falls in love with a young man, gets pregnant, and tries to commit suicide

PROLOGUE

When I came to New York as a teenager, one of the first people to befriend me was a Japanese kid named Toshii D. We were both sixteen and clicked immediately. Soon we were playing sports together, discussing world politics, going to rallies, hanging out, partying, and on our way to becoming best friends. On a cold autumn day a few years later, Toshii stopped by my apartment, looking weary, wearing his usual worn jean jacket, with a rolled-up shirt and his hair in a ponytail. The jacket was too light for the blustery weather, and I told him, but he said he was fine.

This was the fourth time in a week he'd visited, due to his weekly sessions at Columbia University's Presbyterian Hospital, where he received his dosage of Darvon, a powerful painkiller that he was using to assuage the phantom pain in an amputated foot, which had been surgically removed a year after he was involved in a cab accident. The accident trauma also caused Toshii's intense depression.

As he sat and talked to me, I momentarily drifted off, not maintaining eye contact for a second or two. He immediately took my side-glance as inattention and blurted, "You're not listening to me. I'm really useless, aren't I?"

Not knowing how to respond, I told him that he should just give himself some time. Later that night, his mother called and asked if I had seen him. She was worried that something might be wrong. The next day, Toshii's crutches were noticed by a worker on the Staten Island Ferry, and twelve days later he was found floating in the Hudson River.

Toshii's suicide left a lasting feeling of emptiness, of loss, and as I write these words I'm reminded of how dear he was to our families, and of our friendship. In some ways, writing about his death so many years later is almost a kind of betrayal, because I could have written about him before now. Then again, this timing is more fitting because his memory is fresh and our friendship has endured despite the passage of time.

Toshii's suicide note mentioned his love of his family and friends and to whom he wanted his possessions to go. He wrote that his loss of manhood was what really crippled him, and that this was a loss he could not remedy.

But I didn't really believe that. The measure of a person does not come from merely external situations. A lost foot need not drive someone to suicide, nor does a faulty family, a bad job, or a poor school. What makes a person kill him- or herself is the belief that they have no foundation in their lives, from the very start—never knowing that they are loved, smart, accomplished, on the right path, or worth something; never having any of the nurturing that all children need. Then, that confused and fragile mental condition is compounded by external issues that push people over their limit—such as a crippling injury, terrible parents, or an environment gone wrong.

I've met other kids along the way, kids who were like my friend. Some were preteens, confused, lost, and I began working and writing with them—and writing about them, for years. Yet I felt I was missing a very important point. Getting them to start writing, hooking them up with contacts, and shining a light on their ills obviously wasn't enough, because the root of their pain still wasn't being addressed, and this was evidenced by their constant talk of suicide. Every kid has it rough, some more than others. But for all kids, growing up is hard. Learning the lessons of life is hard. All kids are going to have problems with their parents and friends and society and school. But not every kid is going to cut herself until she bleeds. Not every kid is going to tie a rope around his neck. Not every kid is going to smoke pot until becoming completely numb.

I remembered my friend Toshii, and how the roots of his problems had surfaced before his injury, before his attempts at self-help. Maybe if I'd noticed the signs earlier, I could have done more for him. And here they were, in front of me again—signs of suicide in notes, in poems, and in journals—right there on the page, as if these kids were saying, "Look, my problems are right there. Help me!"

This book is about teenagers who, in desperation, rage, anger, depression, or even drug-induced euphoria, either attempted suicide, committed suicide, or injured themselves. This book is written to tell their story and to alert parents, teens, and others about why and how suicide and parasuicide (suicidal gestures or attempts) are more prevalent than ever in our society. All the teenagers profiled in this book felt desperate enough to construct suicide notes or to write in diaries or journals about matters that they perceive as unsolvable, issues that relate to their sexuality, peer influence, bullying, incest, rape, or murder. The real question is why would a teen in the prime of life want to kill herself? I decided to write on the subject to inform readers about a handful of young people I've come to know through the suicide notes they wrote and through the letters, diaries, journals, and poems they penned to family and friends.

I have come to understand suicide not only as a sociologist but also as a father, a mentor, a teacher, and a friend of victims. My best friend committed suicide, and I had a lot of guilt because I was the last person in our circle of friends and family to talk to him. I thought I should have been more sympathetic to his situation, and perhaps should have tried to convince him that life was worth living.

At this crucial crossroad in our cultural malaise, parents and their children need to establish a dialogue that attends to the key problems related to teen suicide: denial and blame. There is denial that we live in a "chemocratic" society in which drugs (whether legal or illegal) rule, and then there is blame, constant aspersions cast against victims. In most circumstances, too, there is refusal to face issues such as suicide and drug misuse honestly.

This is not a fascination with the past so much as a way to show that, although things change, much stays the same. Though today's music is electronic, kids of the rave and Goth cultures still suffer from the same anxieties and problems that kids did back then. In some ways, this work is an homage to a bygone era, but really it is an ongoing account of teenage life and culture.

My research has attempted to debunk myths surrounding our collective denial and constant need to blame the victim. Our failure to confront teenage suicide is one of the reasons I have written this book. Although school shootings have opened the nation's eyes to youth violence and have inspired full-scale examination, denial still shrouds teen suicide. One would be hard-pressed to find an adult in America who does not know a seriously troubled or disturbed teenager, either within his or her own immediate family or among the offspring of friends or relatives. And most of these adults would probably admit that they are at their wit's end in trying to understand a problem that is threatening to tear apart the American family.

During the course of my research with teenagers in New York City's Goth underground, in drug gangs, and in community-based high school organizations, I was struck by a surprising common denominator among the teens interviewed: a serious number had engaged in some form of self-injury. In the aftermath of the tragic events that have taken place in and around American schools in the past few years, citizens have been wondering aloud what's going on with kids. American schools have become the center of bombings, mass shootings, and other carnage unprecedented in our history. At least five schools bear the image of "horror high," including Columbine High School near Littleton, Colorado; Thurston High School in Springfield, Oregon; Heritage High School in Conyers, Georgia; Bishop Neumann High School in Williamsport, Pennsylvania; and Santana High School in Santee, California. In 2012, twenty-two children at Sandy Hook Elementary School in Newtown, Connecticut, were gunned down by a young man one year out of his teenage years.

Despite a sharp decline in youth crime overall, the public expresses great fear of its own young people. In 2000, violent crime by youths was at its lowest point in the twenty-five-year history of the National Crime Victimization Survey; nonetheless, 62 percent of poll respondents felt that juvenile crime was on the increase. During the 1998–99 school year, there was less than a one in two million chance of being killed in a school in America, yet 71 percent of respondents to an NBC/*Wall Street Journal* poll felt that a school shooting was "likely in their community."

In predictable fashion, fear mixed with wonder and guilt has provoked largely reactionary responses. Television journalists have approached the issue of teen violence as a diabolical conspiracy involving music, drugs, body piercing, tattoos, and Satanism. They parade out tattooed teenagers headbanging to heavy metal bands and musical icons, which is indeed eye-catching, but this does not tell us much about teen culture. Such reports also fail to offer an unbiased view from the perspective of teenagers themselves, much less any sociological insight into the underlying causes of teenagers' feelings.

When I was working on the ethnography of crack culture in New York City, desperate teen crack users who could not find a way of ending their addictions often would confess to me that they would like to end their lives. This "pleasurable suicide," if such a term could be imagined, involves the misuse of so-called good chemicals, used in recreational settings over time, which methodically "kill" a person spiritually, emotionally, and psychically. The use of drug-induced highs as a means of suicide is perhaps less painful than more violent methods such as hanging, roof jumping, or shooting. But is this really suicide? What is suicide? Is it the act of taking one's life voluntarily and intentionally, especially by a person of sound mind who is old enough to exercise discretion?

In sociologist Donna Gaines's classic *Teenage Wasteland*, the horrors of suicide are revealed in a powerful story of a group of teenagers in Bergenfield, New Jersey. Gaines began questioning the widespread apathy of teenagers when four committed suicide together. For Gaines, suicide among this age group reflects not the angst of an individual but something more profound and complex, and it is related to a kind of hypnotic draw toward the idea of suicide that many teenagers experience. "For young people, suicide promises comfort, a means to an end, a soothing and delicious deep sleep. In the context of young lives, lived like rapid fire, but focused nowhere, suicide seems thrilling, intoxicating, contagious. Death and suicide become eroticized, as terror and rapture, self-loathing and self-gratification."[1]

These privileged kids had lives that were unfilled in spite of all the wealth and fine living they enjoyed. Something was missing, something that united them all.

What united them all is that they were alone, but through their own words, we get to see deep inside their souls. We're going to be right next to them as they cut themselves and hurt and bleed. We're going to see what they go through, in the hope that their words will shed light on the problem—light that can help other kids, such as my own son or the daughter of my neighbor.

But this book is not solely about uncovering a subject; it's also about giving a three-dimensional picture of that subject. I have always thought it peculiar when kids say and believe things that are so obviously untrue—like when they speak of being completely alone or helpless or totally unlovable. None of these things is true—for anyone—and in these pages I challenge these thoughts with other thoughts that are more positive, creative, and deserving of these intelligent and brave human beings. If someone is cutting herself to relieve pain, I offer a creative alternate solution. If a person feels like the world is coming down, I help explain that feeling, why it's there, and how to alleviate it. If someone feels he can't trust anyone, I place the responsibility back on his shoulders and ask him to take charge of his own life. There are, of course, cases when I have been inclined to seek and recommend professional help for some of these teenagers, in part because some of them truly are alone, bereft of the support system they really need.

What separates the kids in this book from the rest is that they have nowhere to go; no one to talk with; no emotional sustenance, attention, or caring; no direction to turn. They have issues of trust, and since they trust no one, even strangers become easier to talk to. All the problems they encounter—from the simple act of growing up to family abandonment and abuse—gets stuffed inside, with no way out. But those problems can't stay inside forever because they hurt too much. So the kids try to get the hurt out on their own. They cut their skin. They smoke, snort, drink every day. And when things seem like they are going nowhere, they kill themselves and leave letters behind to remind us they once lived.

INTRODUCTION

In the early 1980s, during our research about teens in four U.S. cities and seven communities, my colleague William Kornblum and I began exploring how teenagers survive without working. This research focused on the underground economy and the role teens played in it. I then expanded the work to illegal drug markets, exploring the world of teen drug dealing in New York City. At the conclusion of that effort, I again collaborated with Kornblum, in 1998, on *The Uptown Kids: Struggle and Hope in the Projects*, a book about public housing in New York City, where much drug dealing was rumored to occur, and about the role that teenagers played in the life and culture there. All of this research involved young people from age eight to nineteen.

I next broadened the scope of the research to include a wider range of teenagers, from white, middle- and upper-class kids living in suburban and rural areas, who were emerging as actors in the rave and Goth scenes, to kids who hung out on street corners. It was in this new world of teen drugs and avant-garde fashion that I found young people willing to discuss with me more intimate thoughts about how they were treated in their families.

I discovered that most of the kids I was seeing were like strangers in their own homes, and that element of strangeness had pushed them to the point where they were refusing to cooperate. They were like pariahs, so they had evolved into their own culture of refusal, a new tribal society of totally independent families. To find these kids, and to talk to more who held this attitude, I went to the street, to schools, to the projects and street corner hangouts, and even started a project to recruit kids and learn from them about their ways of thinking and behaving—and I began formulating opinions.

At the time, I was living at the edge of Harlem, in Washington Heights, and kids were just starting to sell drugs openly on the street, which was a new phenomenon. What was interesting was that these kids saw themselves more as "citizen outlaws," giving the public what it wanted, than as criminals. They talked much about the likes of Billy the Kid, in the Old West, or early 1920s gangsters like Al Capone. These kids were searching for an American dream that was historically brought about through illegitimacy. The Rockefellers, the Morgans, the Vanderbilts, the Kennedys, and many of the robber barons got their goods through dirty means, and these kids felt like they were the logical heirs to these men. I started writing about these kids as they were establishing a new kind of crew, which was more like a corporation than anything else, and this research led to *The Cocaine Kids*.[1]

During research for *Cocaine Kids*, I discovered that many girls were falling prey to drugs and were becoming pawns in a much bigger game. They were getting kicked out of their homes, following their boyfriends, giving in to peer pressure, self-medicating and becoming misusers of drugs, and then spiraling out of control until they were performing blow jobs in alleyways just to stay high. In a new book, *Crackhouse*, I tried to explain and under-stand how life had turned upside down for these girls.[2]

While writing *Crackhouse*, I realized that as a scholar and a writer I was constantly talking about people and their lives but that little was actually getting done. I was simply relaying kids' stories and shedding light on the problem; the kids themselves weren't being affected at all. I was using my influence to get their stories out, but for real change to occur, the power dynamic be-tween myself and the kids had to change. I didn't want to exploit them, but I also knew the limitations of appearing as a "social worker" and wanting to "help" them. I had to change the way I was dealing with their problems.

One day soon after my epiphany, I bought one hundred small journals and went into four public housing projects, walking through the area streets. If I saw any kids hanging out, shooting craps or shooting hoops during school hours, smoking blunts on stoops, or if I saw girls with baby carriages, I approached them, gave them a journal, and made a deal. I'd pay them a nickel a line, a dollar per page, to write their life stories and then come talk with me and other kids who had similar stories.

Buying those journals took me to a new place in my life and career. I was no longer just a social scientist writing about kids; I was also taking steps to try to effect change in these kids. I was offering a kind of social capital—basically, a network of contacts that could help them deal practically and creatively with issues they couldn't deal with on their own—by giving them the op-portunity to meet with writers they could talk to, artists, self-help groups, pregnancy hotlines, lawyers, doctors, social scientists, graduate students, or employers. I knew these kids were smart, that they could write and count, but they were struggling with basic questions of identity such as Who am I?, Where do I fit?, Why doesn't the society like me?, and similar concerns.

The journals I handed out also became a way for me to look at kids in a way I could never do before, because all their most intimate thoughts were written down right there on the page.

High school principals and teachers began hearing about this writing project after the Discovery Channel made *The Uptown Kids*, another book I wrote with Kornblum, into a feature film called *Harlem Diary*.[3] Teachers started to send our way kids who enjoyed writing or had an interest in creating narratives. One of those high schools was called City-As-School, and I got kids who were tattooed, pierced, gay, abusive, and "different." They introduced me to the world of Goth, and when I started to attend these Goth clubs, almost everything there had to do with death and/or the lure of suicide. This immediately brought me back to the journals I had handed out for *The Uptown Kids*, and when I looked back on these, I noted that in every single instance suicide and death represented a common theme.

In my friend Toshii's suicide note, all the signs pointed to death. He was finished with life, and every word indicated as much. But the suicide letters I was reading—written by a child on the brink of the act—were more cries for help than anything else, even when the person was dead. And I could actually see the progression of these notes through my work with other kids. It starts in frustration: they ask for help but no one comes, so they get angry and act out, scar their bodies, hang with the wrong crowd, self-medicate with drugs, move away from the family—an endless cycle. And, as in the work of most rap musicians and heavy metal acts today, the keys to these kids' rage and frustration, all the reasons behind what they're going through, are right there in the lyrics, encoded in the message, blaring to be heard.

Toshii's letter forced me to realize that I had never known him as well as I thought, and it forced me to question just about everything—my goal in life, my friendships, and who I was and wanted to be as a person. Did I want to be a friend who couldn't notice when another friend was in need of help? Did I want to move through life simply overlooking the problems that were right before my eyes? What was the motive behind my existence?

The kids' writings and discussions stirred something in me, and that something translated into a desire to better understand the young people around me. Over the next few years, I made it my goal to find kids like Toshii, who felt the same way he had, who felt life was no longer worth living. I wanted to talk to them about why they wanted to kill themselves and to help them find that spark, somewhere in their own lives, so they could see that life is an adventure to be enjoyed, not some constant weight that threatens to crush us with each passing day.

The purpose of this ethnographic study is to provide a descriptive account and analysis of a particular form of human behavior that we all find difficult to imagine, using notes from selected teenagers to record aspects of their behavior in order to construct explanations of that behavior in youth culture terms.

This body of adolescent ethnography includes previous work that both informs my methodology and is a progression to the present study, including my work with William Kornblum on *Growing Up Poor* (1985) and *The Uptown Kids* (1994); my collaboration with Eli Ginzberg, *Does Job Training Work?* (1991); my books *The Cocaine Kids* (1989) and *Crackhouse* (1992); and the film *Harlem Diary* (1995). Ethnographic accounts deal with real human beings, with an emphasis on social aspects of behavior rather than on physiological or psychological aspects. I do not claim any expertise in these latter fields. Rather, I describe and analyze human behavior as I see it and understand it, from the perspective of what my training suggests and the words or explanations given me by those whose lives I enter. In ethnography, I discovered a way to learn about kids from the inside out and to discern the hidden meanings behind their body language, glances, speech patterns, and the like. As ordinary people, we ask questions, inquire about things. That's exactly what ethnographers do, and that is what I did—I asked questions to find answers and make assessments about our world by observing and analyzing the kids' world.

The ethnographic approach and perspective is a personal art form, requiring integrity, stealth, perceptiveness, improvisation, courage, and compassion. Ethnography provides a way for people to tell their stories and for the ethnographer to interpret those stories in a way that renders the participants human. It is a sensitive method, in which the researcher tries to see the world as other people see it. Because ethnography involves attempts to provide a detailed portrait of people in their own settings through close and prolonged observation, I also spent time in the life of the neighborhood, learning about its peer groups, its informal organization, and its social structure as opportunities arose during the course of daily life.

In the city this was easy, but in the suburbs my presence was suspect. Even so, I visited malls and went to churches and town meetings. Inside the family home, my presence often opened old wounds, but more often than not, news of my work helped begin a dialogue about ways parents could deal with kids in emotional trouble.

The most consistently asked questions were "Why do you want to write about our family?," "How will you protect our name?," and "How can we help other families going through the trauma of suicide?" These questions provide a way to establish a dialogue with families and kids about a difficult and challenging issue, but most people want to talk about these issues because they feel it will help them cope with a difficult and troubling matter that many conceal or deny. The life story is key to a good, solid ethnography because at the heart of it all are human voices—with faults and troubles, no doubt, but with triumphs, as well. All of this supports a vivid and full personal narrative about teen suicide, a picture more exacting than one set of categories and more important than any one theory.

In traditional ethnographic work, the researcher chooses a site or finds a location where the research is to take place. In this work, however, the teens in many instances chose me, and I, in some cases, followed them. In other cases, I found teens who wanted to tell their own story or the story of a friend or family member who had committed suicide, or teens who had written about suicide attempts in journals, diaries, or letters. In one example, I was an expert witness in a capital murder case, and, by chance, a teenage boy began to tell me about how he was raped in prison and how this led to his attempt to kill himself. One student came to me because she had an illness, another because she had read about my use of journals in a not-for-profit organization, and yet another because she'd read one of my books, which mentioned journals. Thus, the kids who people this book come from varied and sundry pasts, and as such, the makings of the book are sui generis. All of the voices, stories, and lives of the young people in this book came in these unusual ways.

Some would argue that asking kids about suicide is an enormous act of violence against them, whereas others see the importance of such an inquiry to learning about histories that are unspeakable. An examination of how writing a journal or diary makes the unspeakable speakable is also part of what we are looking at here.

There is minimal "baseline demography" of the young people profiled here. If I were to present such data, however, it would show that the idea of suicide and troubled family life cuts across class and explodes the old myth of the two-parent household as the be-all and end-all of familial models, a subject that is no longer an important discussion today. Even without such data, this fact reveals itself in the narrative.

In the initial stages of this research I spent time with kids from a local high school, some of whom worked with me as interns at The New School; others visited my classes, curious about graduate school and the "professional student life." In the course of our various conversations, I learned about Goth culture and began nourishing ideas related to suburban white kid culture, and this is when the subject of suicide among this group emerged.

Although the university is my base of operations, and I did conduct interviews in my office, I soon ventured out onto street corners; into clubs, poetry bars, and Internet cafés; into suburban homes and high schools; to various hotline organizations; and to cemeteries where Goth kids gathered as places of peace. In keeping with these varied locations, I also employed many research strategies in gathering information. For example, I used a snowball sampling technique, in which I connected with kids who then introduced me to others who had multiple suicide traumas—usually pill popping or cutting. I quickly discovered that most of these were girls, whereas the boys admitted to "suicidal thoughts" while on drugs.

Another approach was to seek out so-called suicide clubs, a phenomenon popular in Japan but relatively unheard of here in the United States. In such clubs, teens join together and write in personal journals and diaries about committing suicide—how they would do it and with whom. I was not able to locate such clubs, but other teens provided diaries and journals for me to read. The main problem was the need to provide or guarantee anonymity to those who were willing to speak or to reveal diaries, journals, and letters, which meant changing names and identities. Given these various constraints, it is possible to lose some detail, but I have done my best to represent accurately both the teens and the families of those who told me their stories.

I visited the gravesites of two suicide victims as a way of paying my respects to those families, but the vast majority of families refused my request for interviews.

In the summer of 1999, I gave several kids cameras and journals as a means to express their views about death in the city, and what they found ended up in an exhibit. I had used this approach before and had found journals useful tools to get kids to tell their stories. Several had used journals, as well as letters, diaries, and other personal narratives, to address themes such as death, violence, sex, body piercing, music, athletics, appearance, and spirituality. One girl of sixteen wrote in her diary about cutting:

> The exacto knife was bleeding like my arm. The blood running off the side, dripping onto the rug. I couldn't move. I just watched . . . Love was my obsession and my weakness. My forearm bleeding and raw, the letters of his name etched in my skin and my heart. I was scared and happy, excited and calm.

An eighteen-year-old boy says with exasperation, "Many kids say we are too wild and 'crazy' in our teens and don't know who to turn to for help."

Sex, violence, music, and death are persistent themes in the lives of these teens, and death is a recurring theme among teenage followers of the Goth scene, many of whom became part of the group I visited here. "We all gotta die sometime," an overly pierced teen told me.

The teens in this book, such as Jill (chapter 8), Cody (chapter 9), and Candy (chapter 3), all either attempted or committed suicide out of desperation, rage, anger, depression, loneliness, or even drug-induced euphoria. The suicide notes they wrote touched on everything that they perceived as unsolvable in their lives, including sexuality issues, peer pressure, incest, rape, and murder. Some are desperate cries for help; others are subtle, rambling passages of remorse. But all are part of a long process—perhaps the last stage of such a process—in which the writers are convincing themselves that they deserve to die.

Two of the more vexing questions I faced in doing this research are what exactly is a suicide note, and why do kids—or anyone for that matter—either commit or attempt suicide. Psychologist Antoon Leenaars offers one answer, arguing that suicide notes are "ultrapersonal documents. They are the unsolicited productions of the suicidal person, usually written minutes before the suicidal death."[4] Such notes are an invaluable starting point for comprehending the suicidal act and/or for understanding the special features of the person who actually commits suicide and what they have in common with the rest of us.

The second question was raised after I received a phone call: "Enoch just tried to commit suicide." This was the message about one of the kids I had been talking to for not quite a year. It was a disturbing call, and I began to wonder why Enoch would do such a thing. For the most part, teen suicide might seem related to unhappiness, dissatisfaction with life, trouble with peers, or problems with parents, but many will disregard the teen's relationship with his or her friendship group. I know Enoch had some problems with school and his parents, and his emotional state undoubtedly played a role in generating suicidal impulses, but I believe such state-of-mind explanations do not explain some more revealing information about suicide.

If we look at suicide rates (the number of suicides per 100,000 people in a particular category), we find that not all people are equally prone to suicide. We know that, historically, males are more likely than females to attempt or commit the act; Protestants more likely than Catholics; single men more likely than married men; people with more education are more likely than those with less education; and soldiers more likely than civilians, according to Émile Durkheim.[5] This raises some questions. Are men less happy than women? Are highly educated people less happy than less educated people, or are Protestants less happy than Catholics? It could be argued that there is no difference in the happiness of men and women, or that people with higher education are, on average, probably happier than those with little education. This would suggest that different rates of suicide among different groups probably cannot be explained by different degrees of emotional states such as happiness. It would also suggest that the reason, say, Protestants are more likely to commit suicide than Catholics must be related to the social meaning of being a Catholic or the social meaning of being a Protestant, although Durkheim's findings on suicide rates among Protestants and Catholics have been critiqued, corrected, and negated many times to present day.

I am interested in these questions, in part, as a seasoned researcher-observer, as the father of a teenager, and as a person sensitive to the concerns facing young people today. At the same time, I am not sure that we can generalize "special features," though certainly as researchers we can provide approximations.

I feel honored to write about the issues young people have revealed to me, which include concerns related to sexual preference, stress, success, emotional and sexual abuse, unplanned pregnancy, unemployment, imprisonment, parenting issues, and leaving home.

Kids live in a world few adults really understand. Their world is one of contradictions, confusion, and ambivalence. The kids in this book are not any different; they represent a continuum, a scale, a range from suicide to suicidal thoughts. Many engage in the ritual of death—such as by dressing in black clothing or wearing skull-and-crossbones jewelry—as if they were acting in a stage play or drama. They all write in journals/diaries about killing themselves, and in these stories you will see a scale, a range of kids who go to the farthest extreme, from hanging themselves to slicing the surface of their arms, faces, legs, and heads.

These are kids who are conflicted in some way or another in their lives and who have some overwhelming obsession or conflict in need of resolution. The issues they face are very real, and most of these kid-related concerns are universal problems. In the case of these particular teens, however, the concerns have become so overwhelming that they can think of no other solution than to die. They choose many tools as weapons to express these feelings—razor, gun, rope—and in each instance their hope is to find the ultimate way to get the last word.

The theoretical, sociological, epidemiological, and ethnographic synthesis that (at this particular time) binds these narratives together to form a coherent understanding of teen suicide is the idea of intimacy, which suggests that the private world of the person inevitably conflicts with the public world of culture and society.[6] Sociologist Robert Merton's definition of manifest and

latent functions also serves as a way to understand what teen suicidal behavior is all about. The journals and diaries have a manifest function in that they serve as an expressive release of individual feelings and pent-up emotions. The latent function is the
coming together of kids with similar issues, including kids who
are suicidal, to talk and to write (as talking and as cure) about
their frustrations, fears, and desires, in the hope that suicide will
not be a reality and that this sense of shared feelings and writing
will act as a form of emotional cleansing.

Epidemiological theories about how disease afflicts specific
populations —why, and by what cause—are evidenced in the various suicide elements mentioned in each case presented here. In
this case, the population is teens and the causes are variously ex-
plored. The most obvious theory relates to embodiment—the
body is dissected in various dimensions as an entity attacked by a
specific form/kind of social dis-ease: parental neglect, sexual abuse,
beatings, rape, or depression. I'm reminded here of Loïc Wacquant's ideas about embodiment and boxing, and the Maussian
notions of body techniques.[7]

In some ways, my ideas about teen suicide are formed by the
research I do and are determined by looking at empirical evidence. There is a great deal of research on teen suicide, mostly
statistical, but almost nothing on the day-to-day realities of teens'
lives and suicide-related issues. Suicide is the ongoing expression
of the conflict between the self and an exterior imposition; more
specifically, it is what the self does not want to submit to or to be.

I believe a little theory goes a long way, particularly when the
personal is linked to the ethnographic as a means of scientific inquiry. These are refracted narratives, drawing on the teens' journals, diaries, and letters and on the stories and accounts told by
friends and family about various situations relating to the teens'

suicide or suicide attempts. All present a striking and disturbing picture. The key to these narratives is to allow their internal logic to speak for itself, without the urge to engage in adult/parental moralizing. I would like to think this interpretation embraces the narratives.

Each of the narratives shares a synthesis, the most engaging of which is writing as a form of technology and emotional cleansing. I have used this ethnographic technique in the past, and all of these theoretical pieces help to frame the narrative construct. One major trope in suicide notes is this: the teenagers who wrote them did not actually want to die. Thus, the suicide notes and narratives represent an organic confession à la Albert Camus: suicide as a confession of anger, angst, disgust with life as it is lived. And this could represent, in a sense, an emotional exorcism or bloodletting.

A logical sequence of queries could be brought to the surface here. For example, we might construct a (theoretical) framework that characterizes teenagers who did *not* commit suicide. Because only two of the notes indicate suicide, such a framework might discern a telltale difference—an actual marker of sorts—between suicide notes from teenagers who actually kill themselves and those who do not. In other words, are kids who leave suicide notes somehow different from those who in fact commit suicide? What do note leavers want when they leave a note but don't commit the act? Other conceptual ideas derived from the text are the ideas of a network of shared feelings and the intergenerational transfer of unresolved trauma. Finally, the idea of teen suicide as a kind of "rite of passage" is perhaps conjectural, but I do find this to be a common feature, based on my reading of this very small sample.

TEENAGE SUICIDE NOTES

1

LITTLE GIRL LOST

Kyra

Kyra, seventeen, wrote in her diary on a regular basis. One entry read:

> I am nobody. Nobody is me. And yet I can't help being me. Can I?
> It's unbearable how long it took to find a way out. I had to laugh
> at myself for being so ridiculous, trying to accept my situation,
> trying to make the best out of it as society's tenor seems to echo.
> Trying for a Prince to kiss me awake like the Prince in the *Sleeping
> Beauty*. I don't just want to sleep, though.
>
> Picturing myself dying in a way I choose myself seems so com
> forting, healing and heroic. I'd look at my wrists, watch the blood
> seeping, and be a spectator in my last act of self-determination.
> By having lost all my self-respect it seems like the last pride I own,
> determining the time I die.

Kyra is a tall, pretty girl, dressed in classic hip-hop style: overalls with the strap buckled on one side, a loose tank top, and
Puma sneakers. She often speaks as if she is talking about someone else, another person at another time, a body separate from her

own. Despite her hard-edged pose, she is vulnerable and speaks in a low, graceful voice. In this voice, she tells me her self-inflicted torture will never stop. She has attempted suicide by cutting her wrists and by starving herself—the twin food disorders anorexia and bulimia have been part of her young life for some time now. Nonetheless, she's tough, smart, and unabashedly honest about the role these suicide attempts have played in her life.

I met Kyra in 2002, and after several meetings in coffee shops and the school cafeteria, I visited her place to see her journals and to interview her more formally. The apartment is in a modern complex with a short elevator ride three floors up. The three-bedroom flat is average sized, moderately furnished, with low ceilings. Kyra's room is a mess—clothes strewn everywhere; magazines piled in a corner; sneakers, books, and crumpled paper strewn over the floor; a zigzag stack of CDs perched precariously on top of a small television set. Tucked on a corner edge of the bed near the window is a neat set of journals, placed on an empty miniature plastic garbage container.

Kyra's room, across from the living room and down the hall from the dining alcove, is separated by a large glass panel window from the kitchen and bathroom, one of two "cutting spots" where Kyra said she wanted to die.

My suicide will be my way of getting over this illusion that things will get better one day. And I know it won't get any better, because I'll still have my same problems and those same problems will always find a way to drag me down. You see, no matter what, I'll still be myself, and I'll still have to deal with the memories in my head. These are my memories of things. I just feel I can't make it any other way. Well, I won't be a bother anymore. And I'm sick of struggling.

She starts twirling her hair, her eyes searching the room, an occasional smile crossing her tiny face despite the gravity of our conversation. She has small lips that break into a sharp smirk every time she ponders a question, but it vanishes just as fast, and she responds with considerable thought.

I can't tell by looking at her whether she's well or not. She has none of the bloated, water-retaining look of a bulimic, nor the emaciated appearance of an anorexic. Her skin is smooth and her weight appears to be normal. On a cool Friday morning, she starts telling me about her "suicide plans."

I had chosen a date. I thought about what the day would be like. I had been depressed for two weeks, and during that time I decided that was it. I would just find a date and do it.

Kyra says this with a matter-of-fact glaze over her eyes. She projects neither sorrow nor glee; more a sense of welcome release.

I wanted a calm day when my mom was around. The weekend before my mom was to go away, so I knew she'd be home for the weekend I had planned it.

So the day came and I was really miserable. My mom sat in the kitchen, looking depressed as usual. I started crying and she said, "Well, what's the matter with you now?" And I said nothing, but her attitude kinda urged me on, so I got up and went to the bathroom. I ran some water, got a razor blade out of the cabinet, and sat in the tub, holding it in my hand, turning it so the light would shine on it, and I started saying to myself, *When are you gonna do it?*

I pulled the stopper from the tub and let the water run out, and I said to myself when the water runs out I was gonna run out too. I would be dead.

I took the blade and made a small cut, and then I said to myself, *Don't be so weak; do it.* So I cut my arm deeper and the blood started flowing, and then my mom knocked on the door and asked me if everything was okay. I didn't say anything, and heard her working the door with the screwdriver, and she finally opened the door and found me in the tub. I told her to call an ambulance.

She just got in and hugged me, and then I started crying again. When my mom held me, it was very bizarre, because she never does that. She called a doctor friend of our family, and he came over and started asking me all these stupid questions, but I didn't say a word. I was silent.

The motivation behind many of Kyra's suicide attempts was both to relieve the pain of the loss of her father and to get attention from her mother, who continually ignores her, wallowing in her own self-pity. Kyra desperately wants attention, but she's also a smart, empowered girl who instinctively felt that killing herself was not a way out but simply a way to die. So she didn't kill herself, but then she felt she still wasn't getting attention, and now she felt she couldn't do anything right, either. This is a case of a brilliant child who continually blames herself for her own misery and cannot find her way out of a problem. Even though such kids instinctively feel that suicide is wrong, they can see no alternative that will help them through a difficult time, especially when they are not getting help from anyone around them.

I don't know whether Kyra's mother suffers from depression to the degree that Kyra does, but I believe she does. A hug and a chat was all Kyra received for her last suicide attempt. After that, mother and daughter fell into the same disconnected relationship as before, and a few weeks later Kyra went back to her anorexic ways and feelings of low self-esteem.

She kept a running diary of her situation, but at first allowed me to read only a small passage: a warning to parents about the mental state of their children. So I asked what signals she gave her mother.

> My mother said she didn't know I was depressed enough to kill myself. She kept telling me she didn't know I was that bad. But that's all a lie, because I kept giving her signs and hints.
>
> First of all, I was practically a skeleton because I had lost so much weight. I wasn't talking. I was very aggressive. I was very snappy. I mean, I just was not able to have a normal conversation with her. I was always fighting with her. My mom was the only person I really snapped at or was really mean to.
>
> How many signs do you need?

At the age of eleven, Kyra was invited to a ski resort with friends, and it was the first time she had been away from her family. She arrived feeling happy and excited about the prospects of spending time away from her brothers and the fussiness of her mother. The first two days went well; she enjoyed herself and participated in the activities. By the third day, however, she started to withdraw and intentionally missed meals.

Feeling uneasy and worried about what others might say, she decided to eat with everyone else at dinner on the fourth day, and she immediately felt ill, vomited, and collapsed in the lounge.

> I just felt so tense that I fainted at the table, and it was kinda a big deal. And since I had never been a big eater, everybody at the ski resort was a little suspicious that I might be anorexic.

When Kyra returned to school, her teacher called her mother in for a talk about eating disorders.

My mom said that I was all right, that I just got nervous around new people, and it was our problem, not anyone else's. But, you see, I considered myself bulimic at that time, though it quickly became anorexia for about three, four years, and it became like a taboo subject around the house, because nobody talked about it.

Kyra's mom never discussed the situation with her, and as a result, it only got worse.

My mom noticed I was getting skinnier and skinnier, but she never talked to me about it. And then, when I was sixteen, I got into bulimia again. And it was really heavy. It was really bad. Things had gotten too much for me and I was trying to find a way out. And then, when I turned seventeen, this year, I tried to kill myself again.

Kyra's mother said she didn't take her daughter to the hospital the previous time she attempted suicide because she feared the doctors "would destroy her with drugs." After yet another suicide attempt, though, Kyra's mom decided it was best to see a doctor. Kyra explained:

They gave me drugs after my third attempt. I was ill. I was paralyzed. You see, they gave me drugs, but it took two weeks to have any effect, really. But for those two weeks, before the drugs kicked in, I was very unhappy, depressed and suicidal. I was angry and crazed for those two whole weeks, until one day I got two kinds of medication. One was to make me happy—it was like a Prozac— and the second drug I took to sleep.

And when I wasn't awake and happy, I was dead asleep. But this was like a brave new world because once the drugs kicked in I was not a problem to myself. I was just drugged up and drugged down all the time.

I was on drugs for three and a half years.

Kyra did not feel that anorexia was the proper pain to inflict on herself, though it did hurt her mother. The hurt had to be more systematic, more exacting, almost like a game in which Kyra would play out the agony, the suffering, so that everyone would suffer, like her, from a thousand cuts.

She next dedicated herself to self-mutilation.

"When I would see the blood, it was instant relief," Kyra tells me, drinking coffee and fidgeting with the cup. She looks at her arm and points to the now barely visible marks where she'd once marked herself with whatever tool was available.

It wasn't just a scar I wanted anymore, and it wasn't just another red line; it was blood. Seeing the blood was a sign of success, because I had made the most out of the situation. I always felt cutting was powerful, strong, thrilling, because I never felt powerful, or strong, but now, with the blood, I felt the power to have the nerve to do something like that.

I first started cutting after I failed a test, because I felt ashamed. I was always afraid of taking tests. And ever since I was ten years old I was afraid to take those tests, because we had to stand up in front of the class, walk to the board, and write our answers. It was terrible. I was petrified. Then, when I would be called on, I would go up and get it all wrong. It got to the point where my neck would hurt from scrunching down to avoid being called on. The day before the tests, I would get cramps, cry, and be so nervous I would make myself sick. It was just horrible.

I hated myself so much after I failed those exams I just wanted to make myself suffer in a physical way.

I would start marking myself across my arm, and then across my legs, and from the marks I started cutting deeper. Cutting myself was the last thing I would do, because I would be in such a state of anxiety with my tests at school, or dealing with my mom, or fed up with the taunting and insults I'd take at school and things like that. I would get into an argument with my mother and that was enough for me to start cutting myself. And it would be the thing I would resort to, and it got to the point where I would cut myself over anything.

Self-mutilation can be a reaction to trauma, anxiety, or a combination of emotional variables. In this instance, Kyra was suffering from anxiety about taking exams, and beginning with these "hesitation wounds" suggests that she may have had no intention of committing suicide with these cuts.

The places I'd cut were very easy, because I'd use the bathroom at school and the kitchen and bathroom at home. I liked the kitchen because it was where all the knives were, and the bathroom because of the tub.

I had been cutting myself while I was bulimic and anorexic, but this time was different because I started to cut deeper, because I just wanted to feel that there would be more pain. I just wanted to experience more physical pain. I just wanted to scold myself. For example, when I would fail a test I would take my geometric triangle and press hard into my arm, making marks over the skin until I drew blood.

I cut myself about thirty times over a long period, with the hope that I would die eventually. I knew if I cut myself enough, and deep enough, I would eventually bleed to death one of those times. I tried to kill myself. It was like the last exit for me, because cutting was for my failures and the final exit was to kill myself in order to punish myself and to punish my mother.

You see, if I died in this way, I would be making my mother and all of them suffer forever, which is what I wanted to do. I wanted to punish myself and make everybody regret what they had done to me.

Kyra's father died in a plane crash when Kyra was three, and she cites this as a crucial event in her life. Though she remembers none of her childhood until she was about eight years old, it was during this period that the family grieved the most. Kyra's mother, a passive, shy person, found it difficult to cope after her husband's death, so she went deep inside herself, leaving Kyra to fend for herself at a very early age. This death affected both Kyra and her mother. It was a traumatic event, but not necessarily rooted in family dysfunction. This is a core trauma, so to speak, whereas in David's case (chapter 4), there is the trauma of his separation from his father and, later, stepfather due to divorce.

Kyra continued:

Since I really never had a daddy I didn't know what it meant to have one, really. I just went about my childhood as happy as any other child. But, by eleven, I became more aware of the "missing daddy" thing. And started my obsession with family photos, looking for daddy in them and that sort of thing. I used to have this thing about pictures of my family, and we would look at them over and over, trying, I guess, to find the memory that I lost. And since my dad died in 1986 and there is this picture around that time, that year, and my mom and my brothers are all standing around with dead eyes and I'm the only one with an expression of, like, glee or happiness on my face, it's obvious I had no idea or feelings about what his death meant. I was just this little lost girl.

My therapist made me go through some pictures with my dad in them, and every time she mentioned my dad I would cry. But as I got older my feeling became more raw when it came to my father. You see, when I was little I would just say, *Oh, daddy died*, and that was it. But when I was fifteen, about two and a half years ago, something like that, I suddenly couldn't talk about it anymore. I'd start crying and get upset every time my dad was mentioned, every time I thought about him.

I guess I was like that because up until that point I didn't even realize I had a dad. And maybe they didn't want me to know anything about him so I wouldn't feel sad about missing him, like they did. Whatever the reason, they never talked to me about it.

Some of the most troubling issues for a child are related to the emptiness left behind by a lost parent, or by a memory or situation he or she cannot fully understand. Coping with such emptiness can even be more difficult than coping with a beating or an argument, because there is no physical manifestation to blame or confront. It's simply an empty hole that needs to be mourned, processed, and understood. Close family members, friends, counselors, or, especially, books focused on mourning and overcoming grief can help a child get out of these black holes of life.

In addition to the death of Kyra's father, there were other things Kyra's mother never spoke about, and Kyra resented her for it.

My mom was so weak, and I resented the fact that she didn't get a life. If she would have just loved herself a little more or taken care of herself a little more it would have been much better. But she never went out anywhere, and she always just sat in the kitchen complaining to us how miserable she was. So I began to feel that we were preventing her from doing what she wanted. We all felt we were a burden to her. At the very least, it would have been better if she talked about it with us, but she never did. She never talked about it.

She was always silent about everything.

I asked what her mother could have done to help her during this period.

If she had gotten her life together by caring a little more about herself. I mean, I don't mean to totally give up on us but, say, one weekend go out and meet somebody, or have a guy over or something. Try and get some semblance of a life. I think that would have made all of us feel like we are not a burden or the reason for her misery.

I didn't want her to sacrifice for me. I didn't want that. I felt if she could just show us how, after losing her husband, that she could find another one. Why not?

If life shits on you, find a way to get back up. You can still go on. That would have been the thing I would have been proud of. But not this self-pity she showed us.

I was hurting myself. Yes, that's true. But I think I was hurting my mom, too, especially when I wasn't eating. I mean, what else can a mother do but hurt when she sees her child refusing food? I was trying to blame my mom. But I wanted my friends and my

family to hurt, to be punished, because I didn't have to care, right?
I was, like, telling them to deal with the pain now.

Kyra's first suicide note is a confused mix of emotions, in which
blame, resentment, joy, relief, and power all converge into wanting to die. She opens the note by stating it's obvious she should
die because she's worthless, and then she states a sharp need
for recognition from her social world: "I am nobody. Nobody is
me . . . Trying for a Prince to kiss me awake like the Prince in the
Sleeping Beauty."

Knowing that we need and want recognition can be a double-
edged sword. In actuality, it proves how intelligent and intuitive
we are—we notice that there's something we are not getting from
the outside world, and we consciously want to know what it is and
to correct it. In a weakened state, though, we can forget our own
strengths and instead look at the need for recognition as proof
that we are weak and unworthy. This paradox produces a further
need to justify our situation, which is why, in her note, Kyra tries
to convince herself that suicide is a positive thing, is allowing her
to take responsibility for her life, and that it would be heroic:

> Picturing myself dying in a way I choose myself seems so com-
> forting, healing and heroic. I'd look at my wrists, watch the blood
> seeping, and be a spectator in my last act of self-determination.
> By having lost all my self-respect it seems like the last pride I own,
> determining the time I die.

But suicide isn't heroic, because the very definition of hero-
ism is courageousness in the face of adversity. Heroes don't kill
themselves. They have bad days, go through incredible ruts, and
can be on the brink of complete loss, but the hallmark of their

definition as a hero is that they keep on fighting, no matter what, to make every day count and to keep striving for a cause they believe in.

Kyra tries to reverse the act of suicide by turning it on its head, changing a "weak" act into a heroic or superior one. But even that logic fails, because it's a false victory—she "failed" in the attempt. So her "victories" have to come in the mere repetition of the act of committing suicide; in the repetition, she continues to get attention, continues to make others suffer, and, most importantly, continues to suffer herself.

But nothing ever changes. And nothing ever gets better. As she put it:

I used to create a situation where I didn't call anyone and my friends would think I didn't care about them so they stopped calling me. And the cycle is repeated. And you are out there like an astronaut, all by yourself. And it's worse if you don't go to school after you've tried to kill yourself, because the act makes you feel weird, and then when you do go back to school, you really feel like you don't belong there anymore. You feel so alone and that you've outgrown everybody. You feel like you've done something that disconnected you from them.

She cleared her throat and talked more about her diaries.

I wrote diaries, and I have lots of them. I would write about how I didn't wanna live anymore or I wanted to die. Writing is my venting device. I have always needed a way to let things out. As a kid, everything is magnified to such extremes, and the world is always so fucking gray and dark, with no real end to problems. Things just go on forever, it seems.

My teachers and everybody would say I write nicely, and that was very good for me. It was also something that some of the kids would be jealous about, because I would make a literary reference and they would turn around and look at me with a snide kinda face.

And after I started to get those looks I just became silent. I wouldn't talk to anybody anymore, not just because I was upset about the looks they gave me or comments they'd make, but because I didn't want to talk about my situation with anyone. I felt weak and pathetic. I mean, my friends started to say, "Oh my God, not again," and so I just became silent.

At the time, I really felt I was someone without a voice.

After leaving a cousin's wedding, Kyra reflected on her own happiness, and even offered some solutions. In the complex suicide world of kids, finding such solutions can be difficult, but occasionally you get the answers from the kids themselves. Kyra talked about ways to avoid parasuicidal behavior.

Am I happy? Well, I guess the answer would have to be no. But I would like to be, which is a different, a more radical change from the way I was feeling a year ago. I mean, a year ago I didn't even want to think about being happy, just being dead. So, from that point of view, I've changed.

Also, I think I would like to say to the other kids who might be thinking about suicide that, if you're talking about cutting, I would tell kids never go to the spots where you cut carrying or holding any tool whatsoever. By that, I mean with a knife or scissors or anything that could be used as a weapon. And if you go to a spot where utensils are, don't touch them. And if you feel the urge to cut yourself, put ice on it, because it kinda hurts when you do that and you can kinda feel the pain.

I also felt the fact that people can see the cut is embarrassing, because one of my friends who saw the cuts on my arm asked me why was I so pathetic. That might not be a solution, but it might embarrass you, because you feel weak, and it might make you want to change from being that way. I always cut myself in the thigh because people can't see there. I can see there, but nobody else can. But I have cut my hands, too, but I know people won't think much of that because they would just think it's an accident.

There is no manual for becoming a parent, and parents' flaws frequently are transferred to their children, particularly in the area of parenting styles around psychological issues. I think Kyra's mother's issues became her children's issues, because Kyra's mother did not really address her own problems in dealing with her children. For example, Kyra's brother refused to go to school for eight years. I suspect Kyra's mother did suffer from depression, given the situation in the family. This single parent must have been depressed about her son's very bold and difficult refusal to attend school, and about Kyra's acting out.

But when parents become "childlike" themselves, when they are unaware of their own issues, or when those issues affect their children, causing the children to act out or to move deep within themselves, parents typically resort to one of three solutions. They may blame the child for bad behavior, avoid the child (and in effect avoid themselves and the entire issue), or try to remedy the situation with cure-all drugs—even when drugs are the last thing a child needs. Unfortunately, none of those things gets to the root of the problem, which almost always lies in the relationship between parent and child.

Although other factors may impel a child to commit suicide, a fractured bond among close family members creates the first wound in his or her early life, opening a cut that can bleed, become infected, and, if not treated properly, continue to get worse with time. Though I have alluded to possible clinical depression, I am not certain about Kyra's mother's mental state, because this is an interpretive rather than clinical analysis. Nonetheless, a couple of issues seem apparent here: the idea of unresolved intergenerational emotional issues that affect parent–child and family dynamics, and the notion of a fractured bond—Kyra losing her father—as a core trauma wound that may underlie Kyra's cutting and suicidal tendencies. These narratives more or less share certain tropes, even while they diverge, and I think that this interpretive analysis has to embrace the variables in this narrative and has to suggest that suicidal attempts always revolve around parent–child dynamics.

Even in adulthood, it's often difficult to accept responsibility for our own lives, to accept who we are, how we got here, what we want, and how best to achieve our dreams and goals. In most cases we don't want to have to deal with any of those issues, because we feel we're owed something in return for the life we've had to endure—for the terrible parents, unspeakable situations, or countless other things that went wrong. So we wait around for the life we know we deserve to come true, and when it doesn't, we get even angrier and more frustrated at the world and at everyone else in it. But at some point in our lives we all need to take responsibility for ourselves and our current situations. No parent is perfect—and some are downright criminal—but life isn't easy. Nor is it fair. The key is to accept the things we cannot change, to work on the things we can, and to look to ourselves for the strength and inspiration we so rightly deserve.

THE FIGHTER

Enoch

Enoch, sixteen years old (soon to be seventeen), from a poor, rural Virginia family, penned these comments in his journal:

> My Last request is that they cut off my steamship round (thigh) and roast it up and everyone who attends my wake will have to eat a piece. And they will have to eat my cooked heart too. Now, if they don't wanna eat my heart, they will have to drink water with my cremated ashes.

He is a tall, gangly boy with eyes deep in the sockets; a forehead covered by long, curly, semi-dreadlocked hair; and a crooked smile that starts from the left side of his face. He describes his race as "white ethnic." He was nervous with me at first, pulling his long, slender fingers one by one, folding and unfolding his arms, tugging at the worn green hoodie, and finally settling down after a few bad jokes about New York. He looked straight at me, drew his eyebrows together as if trying to solve a puzzle, and asked, "What do you want to know?"

He talked about his life and how he wanted to be consumed in death. Like a street rapper dropping rhyme, the poem rolled off his tongue like a childhood memory, flowing easily out of his mouth beneath unblinking eyes, his posture shifting slightly in the chair as his body turned toward the window. I listened and searched for emotion in the journal recitation, but he showed none.

Tear at my heart . . . Obscure pieces of purity lying in the corridor of my soul. I am blackened. When did I let it happen? Perhaps you may have noticed where I placed my goodness and understanding. I'm nothing more than impulse now. Pure impulse. I'm the scrap heap in the hall. The shed of light peering through the crack in my eye.

Light shed on my soul burns, it hurts, bores holes right through. I want to be burnt because what's left is crystal clear and clean. I need to feel clean.

I'm fooling myself. Why can't I just know my feelings? Why must I search through the files of emotion to find myself? I am tired of this endless trek. I ache and I've grown sick of myself.

I can no longer stand to look at myself in the mirror, and sometimes I scare myself by looking in my own eyes. What am I capable of? Why do I feel anger at a simple trace of displeasure?

I am a piece of shit. Maybe everyone should just stop pounding that into my head and shut the fuck up. But how can I expect people to understand my mind if I can't even grasp myself enough to explain how I feel?

I imagine that I will detach and lose it in my years.

Stand up. Stand up and spite everyone. Disappear into the forgotten happiness, where are you? Deserted. I feel alone. Everyone pisses me off. So maybe alone is how I should be. I can never satisfy myself. What an asshole. All I want is to be in love, but when

I am I only want it to end. Darkness. Shadows deep across my mind, my heart, my soul. I can't escape. I run and run but ease is nowhere to be found.

Happiness, where are you?

I want you. I need you. I need help but when it's offered I turn away. I need a touch but I act like I despise it. How can anyone help me if I can't even explain myself? My life is wasted. Everyone's wasted. I have wasted so much time being stagnant. Closing every door that could bring change, doomed to being the same, waking to the same room, the same job, the same people, the same boring life, everyone's wasted.

Happiness I need to touch you. Everyone's wasted happiness. I feel alone. Everyone else is happy. Disillusionment. Everyone is dysfunction. Every time, I'm displeased.

No one is dead like me.

Enoch, in a relaxed moment, looked more satisfied as he waited for my response. When I said nothing, he quickly began to expound on his meaning.

The day I wrote that suicide note, I had a lot of people in my house. Now, these kids were my so-called friends before I had the apartment, but my place had slowly become a place to just hang. So they weren't really interested in being with me anymore. So sometimes I would leave them and go out by myself, and they wouldn't even know I was gone. I began to feel frustrated, and then it really started to piss me off.

And see, that pissed off feeling fed this little black ball in the pit of my stomach, making it bigger and bigger. Then I feel like I'm losing control of my emotions and shit. And not being in charge of myself, although it's not the thing my brain decides to do. That's when I wrote that piece about my ashes.

Enoch's wishes are cannibalistic and dark, but his words speak volumes about the pain he's going through. It's all right there on the page. "Eat my thighs" and "Drink my ashes" suggest a demented reality, and elsewhere he uses poetically framed words like "Whip me if you please, puppet master" that point to unhappiness, self-pity, and sadomasochistic urges. Drug use is apparent when he speaks of "polka-dotted monkey sell polka-dotted happiness to polka-dotted junkies," and "forked tongues scar my face" refers to his parents, who devastate him every time they lie.

Yet the words Enoch sketches in his writing can release pain more effectively than self-mutilation, because it's creative, takes deep inner courage, and involves productive pain rather than bleeding pain. Free-flowing writing is almost always a doorway into our own innermost thoughts and feelings, and once that doorway is opened, it can expel demons and release solutions to seemingly unsolvable problems, without pain, shameful thoughts, or stagnation. A sentence, word, or phrase is all that's needed to start, and it can be about anything—fantasy or reality. The key is to open a door, step into the light, and take control of life. According to Enoch:

> I feel like now I can express my true self through writing and talking to people, but you have to understand there was a time when I couldn't express myself in words and I would end up using noises to express what I felt. I would just grunt, growl, and sigh.
>
> I really have a hard time getting myself across to people, because I have a hard time connecting to people. And the only

reason why I'm able to talk to you this way is because you're a stranger. You see, I have a much easier time talking to strangers than I do with people I know.

This is a curious construction on Enoch's part: the idea that he can talk to me because I am a stranger. I sense that he is able to do that, in part, because I consider myself a good listener and he senses that. In addition, he was introduced to me by a friend he trusts, and he wants to trust somebody else; he wants somebody to hear him out, warts and all. Finally, I believe Enoch, like all the teens I talked with, felt that my writing about them would mean something for other kids who read their stories, and this was their way of contributing something to their comrades in arms: other kids like themselves, who feel hurt, lost, and maybe even forgotten.

Enoch's life is filled with psychiatric appointments, mutilation games, and blood-drinking rituals, but still he fights, and the beauty of his suicide letters is that they say as much about living as they do about death. He's brassy, bold, and obviously trying to find the answers to life that no one else seems to be giving. This was evident even in our first meeting, in New York, around 1999.

Despite deep suicidal thoughts and actions, I don't think Enoch wants to die. This feeling is common among many teenagers, who simply can't imagine any other way to be happy and live the kind of life they dream of. All of the suicide notes and narratives here could be seen as organic confessions, a kind of emotional exorcism or bloodletting.

Albert Camus, in his book *The Myth of Sisyphus*, argued that suicide is essentially a confession that life is not worth living. He has a term for this, "a sense of absurdity."[1] Most of us go through life feeling we can conquer, control, and master our own universe, however small that is. Schoolwork, a job, a relationship—all these things are done for the good and give us meaning and purpose. But then there comes a time when the opposite happens, when we lose the feeling that life is meaningful and purposeful. All is thwarted by the thought that all our actions are somehow without meaning, absurd really, just going through the motions. Life becomes like the life of Sisyphus, who was doomed to forever push a rock up a hill, only to see it come rolling back down again. We are going through the constant motions, grinding, trudging away, with no particular meaning or purpose in life. So why go on? Why not end it?

Holding his hands together as if in prayer, Enoch explains:

I stopped feeling, after a while. The only connection I had with friends was a commonly shared sadness, so I started to do two things: I got deeper into Goth and got back into cutting.

You gotta remember that Goth, for me, was my reaction to a sense of rejection, and I wanted to spite those preppy kids who didn't accept me or my friends. I'd stick pins into my face and growl. This was my way of getting back.

Enoch lives in a small Virginia town, with rolling hills and picturesque postcard views, but he sees the place as lifeless, boring, and dull. I met him in New York City, and says he doesn't live in this "sleepy town" anymore. This despair about what he sees is compounded by what he must deal with every day in his own home, where he says all his problems began.

Ever since I was a little boy, I've been seeing psychiatrists. I remember coming home from school one day and my dad, who worked in a restaurant, had brought home some seafood. But for some reason my mom didn't want it, and this made him really mad. I remember sitting there on the sofa, listening and watching for a minute, and then I turned my back to them because I didn't want to see them arguing and fighting and I didn't wanna get into trouble for looking, either.

I was thinking, *Wow, this is the kinda personal stuff that my psychiatrist would love to hear, but I ain't tellin' him because it's too personal.* My mom was crying and my dad was screaming, and I later wrote a note to myself about the incident called "The Angry Hand."

I've had suicidal feelings since I was eight or nine years old. When I was thirteen, if I could self-mutilate myself to a point just short of death I felt victorious. I've always felt overwhelmed by shit and so I've been hurting myself my whole life. Even when I was in the fifth grade I would go out with friends who said I was crazy and freaky, and I'd show them I could do this or that to myself, like hold my head under water longer or cut myself.

Self-mutilation is usually a symptom of emotional or mental distress, and I believe Enoch was having issues at home. But I chose to talk with him about it only when he brought up these issues or when I read about it in the journals he allowed me to see. I took my time, choosing my words carefully but saying or asking very little of him, and he just told me the story without much prompting at all.

I didn't see Enoch as "crazy" or "freaky." Instead, like many kids his age, he was just trying to figure out who he was—with little help and even less direction. I wasn't sure whether he was wrestling with a question of identity or the reason for his self-mutilation, but I started to think I might find out more sooner or later, either through further conversations or through the hidden journals he once told me he kept.

Skateboarding was the thing, and I became skate trash, with baggy pants and stuff. I didn't have the money to be a total skater, but it felt good to be judged as the weirdest. I was trying to fit in. I was looking for new things, a desire for change—in music, dress, trying to be different. At home I was poor and couldn't hide it, because I had that free hot lunch card, which only poor kids get. I was being picked on all the time, and after a while, that kind of treatment gave me a thrill.

People shouldn't be rejected. They shouldn't be treated like shit and left to rot. When I first got into high school, I had no new friends. My old friends and I hung out in the cafeteria and we'd sit way back in the corner and start shit, scream on the preppies, or fuck with the "trustafarians"—the trust fund kids. These are the kids who had late-model cars and lots of grass and wore Timberlands, Carhartts—you know, those painters' pants—and 411 tie-dye shirts.

And because I was the newest to the scene, the shit end of the group, I'd tell a joke and they'd tell me I was fucking stupid, even though the next day another boy from the trustafarians would say the same thing and everyone laughed. It made me feel stupid, and angry at myself. Why can't I fit in anywhere?

He'd already felt rejected by his family, too many times to recount, as well as by other kids his age whom he wanted to emulate, and so he started hanging around the kids who were just as lonely, angry, and desperate as he felt.

I started to drift away even further, from my group, myself, and who I thought I was. This was the beginning of my self-destructive behavior. I was made to feel stupid again, and I began to act stupid, and that made me fit into a group that was drawn to bad, stupid shit.

A few months before Enoch's sixteenth birthday he began a bizarre ritual of binding himself with cord after school—a kind of ritualistic mutilation. It was the beginning of a period of both self-mutilation and mutual mutilation between himself and his girlfriend. This was also the end of trying to fit in or to be accepted at home, at school, or in the community. Enoch's desire to have friends, regardless of the kind of friend, didn't matter any longer; association with others who would accept him was the key.

The mutilation stuff started from frustration. Like, I would wrap myself up in a power line cord that I found on the street. I tied the rope to a shelf in my room and would spin around until I wrapped my whole body in this rope, up to my neck.

I was so tight and restricted that you couldn't see any skin and I couldn't do anything except wriggle around. I wanted to get rid of all the tension in me.

Once, in the throes of a deep depression, Enoch tried to hang himself with the cord.

I would get really frustrated, mood swings and stuff like that, and I would have a lot of anxiety, and this tight binding would be therapeutic for me. I liked the pain part of it, but not so much the being bound part.

You see, I didn't like being frustrated. I didn't like being anxious all the time, because it makes me feel insecure. It was like the pain from the rope was beating or pushing that anxiety down. I would bound myself a coupla days in the week, until my mom found the cord in my room one day and took it away. Although she didn't quite know what I was doing with it, she saw marks on my body at breakfast one morning and figured something was up.

But what did Enoch's mother think of these marks, and why didn't she do something at that point?

Many parents with suicidal teens become aware of odd or strange behavior in their kids but simply don't react, either because they don't know how or because they don't want to face the fact that they themselves might be part of the problem. This is a typical scenario. Enoch's mother may have been ashamed or simply in denial, which could be a cause of her inaction.

One day, when my mom saw my arms and legs, she got freaked out and asked me what happened, and I told her I fell into a rose bush. She was in denial about it.

She asked me was I okay, I told her yeah, and that was it. I think she was as relieved as I was that she didn't have to do anything. You see, I didn't want anybody coming around, like social workers and that kinda shit. But when I turned sixteen I was determined to stop self-mutilating, because I had built up a tolerance. I started venting those feelings into other things, like poetry, music, and writing.

But the binding made me feel relieved, especially when I'd reach that point when my face would get really hot from so much blood pressure, like when you stand up too fast and get kinda dizzy and where everything sorta turns white except for those little dots in your eyes. That's when I would stop, because that's right at the point where I am about to pass out.

I never passed out before, but the only reason that didn't happen is that I had another person there. I didn't usually do that around other people, but that time I had my friend Carl there. So that turned into a trust thing between him, his girlfriend, my girlfriend, and me.

I stopped doing binding for a while and I didn't cut myself that much, or at least not deep anyways—just these scratches and a cut or two once in a while on my chest. I would do it on those places where nobody could see it.

Enoch looked excited and proud as he recited another of his poems, his eyes staring straight at me from behind an expressionless face, dreadlocked hair with ends in platted bunches, grungy weather-beaten clothes, a drawn look. In that brief moment, it became clear that this was a talented, resourceful, smart, confused, intimidating, scary young man, a self-taught learner with a bruised soul.

Enoch wakes around eight o'clock every morning, shuts off the alarm, stares out of his window, and glances at the sky to see if it's going to rain. Half an hour later he gets up and walks to the living room to smoke a cigarette. He says he does little during this time because of his mood:

> I'm always pissed off in the morning, but I don't know why. Some of my feelings at the time I wrote the notes were as a result of being basically in a real down time for me. Around this period in my life I had developed a close relationship with my friend Carl and his girl, Sylvia, and I liked her and they liked my girl, Tracy. So we became like family. And so whenever it rained really hard and you

had that big crack of thunder we would all get together and go to Sylvia's house.

We started cutting and drinking each other's blood there. Sylvia lived on this nice long street, and there was a small lake over to the left, leading to her house, with a whole bunch of trees. And we'd drink cough syrup, or sometimes Robitussin, or sometimes we had nothing at all. And we'd run down the street from her house, and strip off our clothes as we ran down this road, and wrestle in the lake and freak out or whatever, and Carl would cut his chest or stomach open and we'd all cut some part of our bodies and we'd all drink each other's blood.

The blood drinking brought us even closer together, because it was an expression of extreme closeness, it felt good. It felt erotic. We did lots of drugs, too. The pain was a release of tension, really, a release of bad emotion, a release of energy.

Cutting and blood drinking among these friends was perhaps a bonding rite, and the four of them may have participated in cutting and blood drinking as a form of collective ritualistic parasuicide. This is a peculiar kind of rite, to be sure, but the use of blood in rituals is as old as humankind, because of the power expressed in blood, symbolically and physiologically. We see it still in some religious initiations, such as circumcision; in animal sacrifice for healing; among gangs such as the Bloods or Crips, or brotherhoods such as the Mafia or the Masons. Blood is used to foster bonds of loyalty among a social group, whether to demonstrate joint hatred for and conquest of one's enemies, to heal afflictions, or to set one's relationship right with God. Enoch specifically indicated that he engaged in this behavior to relieve pain and anxiety. But why are Sylvia, Carl, and Tracy doing this? I was not sure whether they were aware of Enoch's emotional state. I also wonder how teenagers transmit suicidal ideas or coping strategies.

For Enoch and his friends, blood drinking was a way to relieve pain and to bring them closer, but it was also the only way they knew how to express those emotions. Talking, hugging, kissing, and feeling comfort and love were no longer options; these teens had long ago become hardened to these forms of intimacy, replacing them with something darker and more closely related to the surface of their problems. Feeling an instant rush of pain was quicker and easier than getting in touch with emotions that could no longer be trusted (like intimacy and love), and bloodletting was a rush that at least symbolized their level of commitment, fearlessness, and torment.

The rain made us feel powerful, and even today when it rains I get this rush of adrenaline. I grew my fingernails long and I would rip open my chest, scratching until it bled all over and you could see all that red, spotted skin. The first time Tracy and I got together, we started fooling around, kissing, choking, drawing blood, and fucking.

Sylvia would choke Tracy, or Tracy would choke her, and all of this would be a bonding thing.

It was the first time I got off, and the first time I had sex and an orgasm together. She would choke me until I was almost blue. We were both fucked up all the time.

We never hit each other. I knew she was into s/m [self-mutilation], Wicca, asphyxiation, and blood stuff too. She had long fingernails and had cut her legs with razors and I asked if she could show me.

But Sylvia was more private, even mysterious about what she did sometimes. She wouldn't even turn on anything except dim lights in her room, she was so private. But Tracy and I talked all the time, so if I had something on my mind I would talk to her, and if she had something on her mind she would talk to me. But this whole blood thing was about having a feeling of closeness.

I would hug Carl and hold him and stuff, but there was never any real sex or anything between us. It was a brotherhood type of thing.

There are times when kids feel other people do not understand why they want to kill themselves, because it is so irrational and such totally unacceptable behavior. As a result, kids who do understand that feeling will connect with each other, because they feel they know what the pain is. They then connect physically and help each other psychologically, and through this emotional sharing they try to comfort one another. Doing this helps them to find meaning in their own lives as well. The blood drinking becomes a way of sharing their pain, sharing their sins, comforting themselves, affirming their ties.

I'm desensitized now to all the cutting and scratching, and it's true for all of my friends now, too. It reaches a point where the cutting and the asphyxiation doesn't do what it's supposed to do. I would bite down on my arm until my teeth break through the skin, and that was more than enough for a while, but now it does nothing to me. It's like alcoholism—you know, you start with the six-pack, then a twelve-pack, and sooner or later you drinking a case a day. It's pretty much the same thing. As I think about it, I'm glad mom eventually took the cord away, because I would have kept pushing it and pushing it and staying longer, until I died.

But I didn't stop altogether, because I discovered one night while having sex with Tracy that we both like to get violent.

This [choking] with my friends was done when we were, like, intensely involved in the sex. I never really bit or choked my girl much because I wasn't really comfortable doing that to a girl. Her biting and choking me was no problem for me. It just seemed kinda wrong in my mind, you know, like, hurting her.

I never saw this as sadomasochism or anything like that, either, because we never did bondage type stuff. Though we knew that we each liked it, so part of it was to please the other person and to help them subdue whatever feeling they wanted down. We kept cutting each other, drinking each other's blood, because we were in love with each other.

Finding ways to deal with childhood trauma and issues of hurt that get trapped inside them is a continuing problem for a young person, and in some cases those emotions stay bottled up, because the disturbing experience runs too deep.

"The only reason my family moved out here in these woods is so nobody could hear me scream when my father fucked me up my ass."

Enoch made this comment nonchalantly, almost carelessly, before placing his hands near his mouth as if to shut himself up. But sadness covered his brow, as if a bad thought had raced through his head, and though the words were said without particular emotion, the expression in his deep-set eyes revealed something else: the need to tell a secret, to release something held back.

The comment shocked me to the point that I didn't say anything, either. I hesitated to ask him about it or to suggest that he explain further, because I just wanted him to say more. He looked sheepishly at the floor and then said, "I know a lot of kids in those woods would say the same thing. We can't pretend it never happens because it does."

Finally, I summoned up enough courage to pursue the issue. I asked him whether he wanted to talk about it.

Well, I should have said *parents* move out here far away from everything so nobody could hear them when they fucked their kids, because it's not just fathers. That's something I don't want to talk about with anyone. Yes, I said that, but I'm not gonna say any more about it.

The comment confused me. I couldn't figure why he'd say such a horrific thing if he didn't want me to respond in some way. In trying to change the emphasis, he made an even more dramatic statement, suggesting incest by both parents. It made me reflect on the theme of rape in cases where the parents have been engaged in such acts with their children.

This is a kind of "tiered trauma." It is deep, so the emotional state is akin to the ocean—there is the surface, and then there is the deep blue sea. Emotion exists at all levels. In his narrative, Enoch seemed to outline such tiered traumas, and to hint at a kind of unspoken reality that the suburbs (a "gilded ghetto") have their own particular pathologies, which are not put on full display in American life because the people in such communities are considered to be model citizens and to have greater collective value.

Rape victims are so badly violated that they have trouble comprehending the very meaning of their individual space and boundaries. After having their sense of self compromised and being totally subjugated as human beings, it's normal that they should feel completely lost and out of control and experience feelings of disgust, shame, anger, rage, and horror. When the rape victim is a child—someone just starting to understand life and his or her place in it—crises of self-identity only worsen, and professional help is essential. If a rape victim is not allowed to release the feelings that arise from her encounter, those buried feelings only get worse, eventually coming out the only way they can—through intense depression, self-mutilation, drug and alcohol abuse, and, in the worst cases, suicide. The release of such feelings is part of a formal process in psychotherapy and counseling. I believe Enoch's suicidal tendency was inextricably linked to being raped by his father. To me, this appeared to be the core trauma.

Enoch's face was ashen and he looked hesitant, as if he were trying to drag out of himself, with great effort, something that he didn't wish to remember. He moved his hands nervously around his body, pulled his hair, rubbed his nose, crossed his arms several times, and spoke with a distant look in his dark eyes. He had been reading from his journal, or at least selecting pieces to discuss with me. The journal, a rolled-up spiral notebook, well soiled and scratched up, was not the one I'd seen previously. I wondered if this was one of the secret journals he had told me about.[2]

As time continued to tick away, he finally spoke about a sentence he said he had written a while back—I assumed he meant before high school. At first haltingly, then almost inaudibly, he read, "I guess what you feel is better than what you say or even what you do sometimes . . . right?"

He was clearly ambivalent at this moment, wanting to talk about this striking line from his journal but not wanting to reveal the source of so much pain. He wanted me to say something, but I wasn't sure what to say. At last, he explained:

When I first wrote that, I didn't really think I'd keep it in my journal because I thought they [his parents] might find it, so I kept the journals buried in the back woods. I'd almost forgotten I'd written that line. But that's what happened to me, and I was no different than Sylvia and my other friends. Sylvia once told me her father had fucked her, and her mom knew her dad was doing it all along and didn't care. We all came from messed-up families. Carl was really close to his mother and they got along well, but his dad did bad things to him and his mother. His dad molested him just like Sylvia's dad molested and abused her, up until she got her period.

When we bury deep family problems, because we are unable to deal with or discuss them, they never stay buried for long. Many teenagers want to understand and talk about these problems; they instinctively feel that something is wrong. But often they can't discuss it, due to personal shame, not knowing who to talk to, or not knowing what to say. Eventually, then, these buried feelings come out the only way they can—through anger, self-mutilation, acting out, rage, and in the worst cases, suicide.

Enoch continued:

> Sylvia's mother was completely crazy too. I mean, she was committed crazy, and her grandmother was crazy, and her great-grandmother was crazy, and all the women in her family were committed crazy. Now, that made Sylvia very paranoid about herself. She kept looking for signs of this "crazy gene" affecting her. She had this big fear of going crazy.

I see this as an important question about mental health in families—an intergenerational concern. More specifically, it raises questions about how unresolved emotional issues or traumas get passed down from one generation to another—not necessarily at a neurological level but behaviorally. I did not want to delve too much into this issue with Enoch, and I let it pass, but he finished the conversation by saying:

You know, looking for signs that she may be going crazy, I guess that's kinda the sign right there. 1 mean, you know, looking for crazy signs all the time makes you kinda crazy, right? I haven't seen her for a while, and I guess she must be real crazy by now.

Enoch's voice raised slightly as he continued, with an intense look on his face:

Now, my father was very much the same way as their fathers. He was a serious alcoholic and a totally insecure guy who hit me all the time. Now, all the time this [depression, anxiety, drug taking, and binding] was happening to me, I just thought about my dad, who beat the shit outta me all my life. So shit comes down on me and I come down on it. I just stopped living with dad around. He's a big angry fuck who runs the house.

The only time Enoch stood up to his father was one night when Enoch, arriving late after having had a few beers, egged his father on. "He'd told me never come home after twelve or he'd beat my ass, and this night it was after twelve."

He found his dad waiting for him at the front door.

"*Well*, I said, *here I am*. As soon as I got to the steps, he pulled me into the house and kicked me across the room."

In his journal, Enoch wrote:

Alone. I feel overrun by some stagnant grief. When did I become so sad? I wasn't always this troubled was I? Not that there are any

cares left any way . . . Fears and doubts have crept inside my Wall.
Pushing me to the ground . . . Backing me into the dark corners of
my mind. The dust has grown so thick here.
I can hardly see stains on my soul.

Enoch, after several years of cutting and self-mutilating, decided to use his journal as a kind of writing cure. His strategy is intensity and creativity and his focus is on writing journals to stay alive. He's a fighter. Letters, diaries, and journals often reveal to us the diarist's dolorous and desolate pain as it unfolds in his or her daily life. Writers such as Franz Kafka, Virginia Woolf, Sylvia Plath, and William Styron all etched suicide as a central theme in their work-journals. Styron, whose daring memoir *Darkness Visible* deals with his own deep depression, wrote about his revisit to Paris, after many years away, where the illness had first manifested.

Only days before I had concluded that I was suffering from a serious depressive illness, and was floundering helplessly in my efforts to deal with it. I wasn't cheered by the festive occasion that had brought me to France. Of the many dreadful manifestations of the disease, both physical and psychological, a sense of self-hatred—or, put less categorically, a failure of self-esteem—is one of the most universally experienced symptoms, and I had suffered more and more from a general feeling of worthlessness as the malady had progressed.[3]

We know that suicide notes are basically communication about a situation that reflects the mental anguish the person is experiencing. Enoch's suicidal thoughts were not fleeting, nor were they always desperate, but they were chronic. He'd had such feelings, on and off, since age twelve, and he had made a number of suicidal plans and attempts throughout his young life.

Enoch bought a used car, broke up with his longtime girlfriend, and left home to go on the road, as his friend Cody (chapter 9) had done a year earlier. Enoch felt that traveling was one of the ways he might resolve some of his problems. Today, his thoughts are on life and his future.

> Right now, I spend a lot of time in the woods and I'm not as depressed as I used to be. And I guess the only things that matter to me now are the basics, like how I can get from one place to another. How will I get the money to eat today? How will I get the gas to put in my tank? I guess life comes down to the simplest things if you look at it right. I wouldn't say I'm the happiest guy in the world, but I'm certainly not the saddest.

After Enoch finished high school, his depression continued for a time, but he said he just "grew up" and stopped the "silliness." I believe the writing and the talking during all his years of therapy helped, and I think his creative outlets in writing helped alleviate pain in the same way that kids use self-mutilation—but in a creative, healthy, and more focused way. It helped Enoch clearly gauge how he was feeling.

I am not sure whether leaving his hometown and his family house and traveling on the road put Enoch on a path to redemption, but reflecting on his suicide days, he says, "The only thing I'd change from those years of depression and suicide attempts is I'd alter my name and identity and be someone else."

3

OVERLOAD

Candy

Candy, who died at the age of eighteen, once wrote a letter to her friend:

> April 20, 1999
> Dear——:
> To let you into my thoughts/feelings/soul makes me feel vulnerable/scared/lost.
>   I guess it's a self-protection because if I open up my heart for you to read you might find out that you are already there even though you're not supposed to be and if you leave while my heart is wide open you will be leaving me to bleed to death.
> Candy

On the outside, Candy played the part of a normal high school student. She was pretty, athletic, involved in the band and chorus, an honors student, college bound. Few would imagine the complicated web of events that would lead to her suicide three weeks before the junior prom. Her death rocked her small rural upstate New York community and left everyone trying to make sense of a tragedy, the guilt creeping around the edges.

Candy's best friend, Megan, tells Candy's story, speaking about boyfriends and betrayal, virginity, lesbian love, and family squabbles. Candy's story is complicated, as close to a detective story as I encountered during this ethnographic work, because the clues left behind after her suicide—the note, the drugs, and the gun—conjure as many questions as answers.

Childhood is hard enough on its own. It is a world where we are completely beholden to our families to teach us how to live and survive. Abuse in a family is doubly confusing to a child, who is already trying to understand and function in a new environment. Reluctant to blame a parent on whom they rely for nurturing and support, these kids often blame themselves, taking out their pain, fear, and frustration on school systems, other family members, and, in the majority of cases, themselves.

One rainy day in New York City, Megan called me, suggesting we meet for dinner. She said her mother was very eager to meet me as well. Megan, her black hair pulled back, the round glasses covering a face that was brownish with fatigue and lined with worry, stood at the door to her tiny apartment. Megan is a seventeen-year-old Chinese American who lives in New York in an apartment her parents got for her to live in while she is attending school. Here, I was able to meet the other kids in her "family"—Megan calls them a family of misfits. I don't know how Megan became the matron of this group, but she was, and she got all of them to let me see their journals.

Candy and Megan grew up in a small, one-stop-sign town whose top attractions are an ice-cream parlor and a biker bar and where the only doctor makes house calls. Both girls dreamed of coming to New York to attend school.

"Candy and I each kept a diary all our lives," Megan says. "But Candy's death changed everything for me, because writing took on a new sense of urgency."

Candy was a jock. She was a tomgirl jock with real long hair, and she had been a tomboy/girl all her life. We used to climb trees together. She was extremely good at sports. She was in the band, in the chorus. She was an excellent singer. Her hair was a big deal, because you never realize how much hair means in high school. But she was very strong for a girl.

You see, tomgirls are girls who like boys but play with girls and do boy things, like cut wood, ride horses, climb trees and play football and wear pants, but never anything with frills, like dresses. They speak out of turn, hunt and shoot, and fall in love with girls and get raped by boys and beaten by fathers, while mothers stand by and watch and say nothing. You gotta remember that, out in the country, mowing lawns, chopping wood, hiking, all of that stuff, builds muscles, whether you are a girl or a boy. So she was very strong but also very stoical in a lot of ways.

Although Candy was physically strong, Megan felt she was easily hurt by "very tiny things." Megan intimated that Candy had told her she wanted to "die beautifully," but the wish to die beautifully ended with a gun on her father's bed, because the anger at her father grew louder every living day.

There was definitely something physical going on with her father at home, because she would come to school with these bruises on her face. And since my sister and me had never been beaten by our parents, we thought this was odd for her to have fights with her dad. So we'd ask her what happened and she'd say she got into an argument and yelled at her dad and he hit her, knocked her down with his fist. This was so foreign to me, because this wasn't my reality at all.

Sexual abuse by Candy's father was never fully established, though it was implied. Megan wrote a powerful letter to Candy after Candy's death, and though Candy's father is not mentioned as the culprit, it is obvious to all that this is what drove Candy to the final act.

"Anyway, we lived close to each other and she and my other friends would come over to our house and they all liked to talk to my mom. Candy started to talk to my mom, too, telling her stuff about her home life."

Megan's speech started to slow, and a look of sadness covered her face for a moment. She stopped speaking altogether, an indication of how she felt about the beatings her friend took. Megan knew the beatings were the reason for Candy's state of mind at the time of her death, and she expressed this all without saying another word. When she did speak, she offered explanations for the states of mind of all the kids in her "family":

So much is going on in your body, from hormones to religion at this time, it's no doubt kids are confused and shit. Now, around this time (fifteen, sixteen), Candy had gotten through the guilt of smoking pot, the guilt of lying to her parents, the guilt about the sex-before-marriage thing. She had gotten to a place where she was coming out of teenage troubles in a way.

She was one of the few of us who really knew what she was going to do after high school. Around the time she was thinking about suicide, she was coming to visit me, because my family and I had moved to another state. During one of those visits, she told me she was gonna kill herself.

As far as I know, there was no police investigation at the time of Candy's death, though there was one later. Conversations with Megan's mother revealed that Candy's father was part of an exclusive, macho, all-male club of firemen, police officers, construction workers, and mailmen in this small rural village, and this meant nothing would be done; this all-boys club would not inform on one another. This might explain why there was no police investigation.

"We talked about [her suicidal thoughts] briefly, but nothing came of it. I think the last thing I said was that she had too much to live for, something like that."

A week after this conversation Candy decided to have a party while her parents were away. The night of the party was quick, because everything happened very fast.

Candy called me three times the night of the suicide. She scared me, because she kept saying the guns were calling her, and I couldn't understand it. It was May of her junior year, and she was about to become a senior the next year. She had worked through so many demons in her life, but there was something she couldn't exorcise. There was something that was so devastating that she couldn't find an answer to. Something so horrible that she just couldn't shake.

What could that have possibly been, where religion, talking with my mom, drugs, alcohol, her mother, her father, her teachers, her counselors, her friends couldn't help her overcome? Find the answer to that question and you'll find the reason she killed herself.

But anyway, I asked her to let me speak to one of the guys there, and I told them to go and take the guns out of the cabinet—because Candy had her own rack. So they were in the process of doing that. They couldn't get the rack open, so they dragged the whole thing downstairs and locked it into the bathroom. After that Candy called me again and said the girl (Liz) didn't want her anymore and wouldn't come into the room with her but she was gonna try to talk to her one more time. Meanwhile, Candy went into her father's room, laid down on his bed, put the gun in her mouth, and pulled the trigger. If you ask me what kind of statement that is, I would say that's pretty metaphorical.

Candy was a silenced young woman, held fast by certain male oppression in her home, an oppression that eventually became too much to bear. I may be overjudging here, but perhaps if Candy's mother and father had been more like a mother and father—a family that was willing to stand by her and protect her—her life would have been different.

I think that Candy had no choice but to deny her own autobiography, because her reality was too dangerous to admit while still under her alcoholic father's roof and hand. My hope is that by bringing forth her story, piece by piece, that we might somehow unglue the silence that destroyed my dear, dear friend.

Candy and Megan, like so many of the other kids profiled here, used their diaries as a kind of writing cure for what ailed them. It was the nightly diary writing that provided them with a way to get the secrets out and bring the anxiety levels down. Megan explains:

Writing was our way to vent, for sure. But this is not about me but about Candy, and I want you to make that clear when you tell her story. The diary writing was a way to express what we were feeling, and by writing, I didn't have to waste energy or hurt people. Just across town, while I was getting "time outs," from my parents, Candy was getting beaten by hers.

In her own diary, Megan wrote:

Dear Diary:

Suicide starts with small rushes of insanity then passes into a series of desperate action. Candy was smart though. She had been covering up the physical and possible sexual abuse that was happening at home: of course she could slide around all of our concerns.

Discontent with herself. She draws blood and laughs. Stumbling and falling every movement feeds her addiction. The dim light fades and dies. Rain begins to fall, but she is gone as love finds her in a dream.

Her ultimate decision to end her life using her father's shotgun shows a psychological attachment to the violence played out in her body throughout childhood and early adulthood. This was not only confessed in her writing, which she later burned, but also through her self-mutilatory tendencies that I witnessed that day in my brothers room.

Megan suggested that Candy's "small rushes of insanity" and "desperate actions" were caused by physical and sexual abuse both at home and at the hands of boys Candy had the bad luck of being attracted to. As Megan said, "She had a tendency to fall hard and fast, which made love almost obsessive." In her diary, Megan explained:

Candy, one of my best friends was living in a house built way out in the woods in the middle of nowhere. No one hears her when the heated arguments erupt between her and her father and even more importantly, no one was around to ask questions when these fights, these punches, left Candy angry and silenced. She called tonight to confess her pain, to proclaim her frustration.

This reference to woods, also mentioned by Enoch (chapter 2), is interesting as a matter of geography. There are, I assume, fewer witnesses in the woods. But isolation alone does not mean anything. Amanda Berry, Gina DeJesus, and Michelle Knight were kidnapped and held for many years on a suburban street in Cleveland, right next door to people who claimed they did not see anything unusual. Respectability can also be a woody mask at times.

In another diary entry, Megan wrote:

Candy's heart is sore and it hurts me to see her going through so much turmoil alone and unsupported. The —— family is so strict, so catholic, a prescribed set of beliefs, and a rigidity against which I had never had to rebel. Each time she cries I felt the walls of repression. She was at a point of transition. Two years earlier, before I moved to New Hampshire, Candy and I had been together often.

She scared me on a regular basis with her sometimes violent, extreme reactions of self-destructiveness. A case in point. I found her sitting in one of the side rooms in my house during a party isolated from the swarming group of high school freshman. She looked up at me with a blank expression, the exacto knife still in motion. Love was her obsession and her weakness, her forearm bleeding and raw, the letters T-I-M stark against her pale skin.

"Candy," I screamed helplessly, years of living as a therapist's daughter falling helplessly to the emotion I felt at seeing Tim's name written in her blood. In retrospect, that was a warning sign, plain and simple, spelled out for me. At 15, if I'd known that suicide is like a rock falling down a cliff gaining speed and momentum until it hits bottom, maybe I could have done more for her.

Megan's mother told me:

As a social worker, I have a license to protect. Candy was about fifteen years old when she confided in me. She came in from an overnight campout with Megan and other kids one Saturday night. I was making pancakes for about eight or ten kids there in the kitchen. And Candy starts telling me things. She told me that her father beats her with a closed fist.

I could see some scratches or cut marks on her, too. Now, Megan had already told me Candy comes to school with these bruises, and I asked Candy if she thought her mother knew about the beatings?

She told me her mother never hears when her father beats her, because her mother is asleep. Meanwhile, I heard later that Candy had been carving in her arm more deeply and, I'm not sure how, but Megan and her friends believe that the father might have been sexually abusing her as well. I don't have any proof of that, so I shouldn't say anything about it.

Megan's mother said that she had to protect her license as a social worker, but I wasn't sure what that meant. When I asked, she said something to the effect that she should not make false accusations that could not be proven. I wanted to know at what point could she report Candy's abuse to the police or the relevant authorities, and she said, "When I have solid evidence, or if the person accused would be able to testify to the truthfulness of the accusations." Something, by the way, Candy was not willing to do.

Some general family factors in suicide among kids have been identified, such as family situations that are aggressive or chaotic, including physical abuse by parents, and alcohol or drug use by either parent, but especially by the father.

I asked Megan about the sexual abuse charge, and she was adamant.

Candy never said anything about being sexually abused by her father or any family members to me. I don't want her memory tainted by that accusation. Please don't put that in your book. If you must write about it, say what I'm telling you right now: Candy was not sexually abused by anybody in her family. But I do know older boys sexually abused her, and that was the source of much of her problems.

Despite Megan's insistence, I was not sure how she knew with so much certainty whether Candy was sexually abused by a family member. However, I will take her word for it, since she was so close to Candy.

Megan did say that Candy was raped, and she told me Candy didn't start talking about suicide until after this event.

There was this boy who raped her at a party one night. About six months later, this same boy went off to college on the West Coast. He heard about Candy's suicide and wrote me a letter asking if he was the cause of her killing herself.

I don't know why Candy didn't report the rape, or why Megan didn't make a report to the police either, but it seems in keeping with the classic story of a victim being put on trial and being ostracized as a "whore" in a local rural community. This has happened over and over again, and perhaps this is why no one dared report the situation. Candy had admitted to taking drugs and drinking, and this may have left her feeling vulnerable to charges that she had enticed the rapist to act.

Candy would get depressed because of her rejection by boys, and she sought religion as a way to assuage the internal turmoil she felt. She was struggling with her sexual identity, and her religious teachings reminded her that she might be going in the wrong direction.

She would say she was "sinning" after a night of drinking and drugging. You have to understand that the drugs and alcohol took on a sinister side because, instead of weekends, it became an everyday thing. She would go to church after a night of partying and confess her sins. By the time she was sixteen she had done nothing bisexual but was thinking about it. But she told me she was worried about how God felt about it.

She was still having random sex with boys in party situations. She was definitely escaping something. After the rape by this college guy, though, he was the last guy she ever had sex with.

In her diary, Megan explains:

Her tendencies to fall hard and fast made love almost obsessive. Where Tim had been the object of her affection at 15, Liz was who she was swooning over at 17. The memories I've accumulated that lead up to Candy's final act of desecration, flow orderly, one after another in my mind, sometimes gaining momentum and flooding my world.

I remember small details, for example, the empty laugh that sent chills down my spine as it erupted from her mouth, telephone wires serving as our only connection that night . . . The summation of all the memories would be easier to deal with if they were cataloged and clean. Waves of emotion hit me when Candy finds her way into my head in matters that seem suspiciously suicidal.

Both Megan and her mother provided versions of events leading to Candy's suicide. Megan explained:

So, after Candy's parents found out that my mother had narked on them—you know, my mom told her supervisor, the supervisor then informed the police that an abuse case (physical abuse and possibly incest) was going down in Candy's house—Candy wasn't allowed to come to our house anymore. She still came over but just didn't tell her parents.

Like any two people who have spent a lot of time together, Megan and her mother share complementary thoughts one minute and contradictory ones the next. Megan's mom said:

Now that I think about it, my mistake was reporting the incest accusation without any real proof. Because I did report it, and the Department of Social Services investigated it, and everybody denied it, including Candy. But I figured she denied it because she had to go home every night and was frightened. Anyway, her dad is one of the good ol' boys in town and works for a big [construction] firm, so it was a whitewash from the beginning.

So although there was a social services investigation (and family denial in the wake of an investigation), there was no mention of Candy ever being examined by a doctor to determine whether there was physical abuse. This would seem to be a classic case of a failed intervention.

Megan's mother was particularly concerned about Candy cutting herself, because, as she explained:

The cutting is more like—self-mutilation and having to do with kids who usually feel that it relieves them, and also that it's a physical manifestation of an emotional pain. It's a way to manifest the pain that they can't otherwise deal with, because they don't talk about it.

As a licensed social worker, Megan's mom was sure of her diagnosis, and she was animated in her efforts to convince Megan and anyone else who would listen as well.

I think that Candy cutting herself is often a symptom of borderline personality disorder. And borderlines mostly get to be that way through pretty serious abuse at an early age of their life. For example, if you get war trauma when you're sixteen or twenty, you don't necessarily develop a borderline personality disorder. You'll develop post-traumatic stress disorder instead.[1]

Self-mutilation can be a precursor to suicide itself, one of the emotional building blocks or signs. It is clear to me that the architecture of suicide in Candy's narratives—and those of Enoch and Kyra as well—all share certain parasuicidal traits, as the diary and journal notes indicate.

Megan's diary also underscores a network of shared feelings among teenagers that is consistent with the feelings of teens I have seen over my career. Megan is documenting the parasuicidal traits of Candy as a refracted suicide note. This is significant, and it raises many questions about "who knows what" among teenagers, and where evidence of a potential lead-up to a suicide may exist. In addition, teachers, social workers, and other professionals who come in contact with children and teenagers must be trained to spot signs of trauma and physical abuse. The professional protocols and standards about this are not really known. And what is the relationship between a diagnosis of borderline personality disorder and cutting? It is obvious from these diaries and journals that there certainly is one to account for. This is a result of early abuse, usually, and it's a pretty common symptom. It goes all the way from people, say, tattooing and piercing up through cutting and/or branding.

Candy's cutting began with small scratches, then slits, then more severe gashes on the arms. And although no tendon or artery was ever cut, Megan felt it was only a matter of time.

Anyway, all of this was taking place in their house. They have a very isolated house. And sometimes people, if they drink or whatever they do at night, they might just go to sleep and never hear it. Her father could depend on this. I don't know. I don't know that much about what her mother did, but how her mother could not know that Candy was cutting herself and her father was beating her, and it's been going on for years, is beyond me. I could see when she came to school the small cuts and bruises getting bigger and more severe.

The cuttings got deeper and more numerous and showed Candy's desperation. Megan never explained why she didn't call the police or an adult, but the scars were building up to something more dramatic. Megan explained:

The night Candy killed herself, Jill and I had been talking to her on the phone, off and on, for about two hours. You see, her parents had gone away for a week or something and she was having a party at their house and it was like a heavy alcohol, drug-taking party.

That night she was quite loaded on alcohol and other stuff. Maybe she had been doing coke, too, but when she started talking about the guns I got scared and asked to speak to some of the guys who were there.

I told them they had to get that gun rack out of the house, because Candy was talking about the guns beckoning her. Candy was a hunter. Her father had taught her to be a hunter. He had given Candy her own gun rack, and that night the boys at the party did take that gun rack out, like I had asked them to do.

And there was a whole other lesbian thing going on, which I think that Candy was involved with or had been involved with, where she was becoming lesbian or was experimenting with lesbianism, and had tried to get one of the girls and had been rejected by her at the party.

She wanted that girl to come in and hang with her, and that girl wouldn't. It was some other subplot, which had to do with feeling rejected in romance, which I think is probably one of the highest reasons that teens commit suicide. So there was that going on, and besides which, if it was a gay relationship, she was Catholic and it was a small town. Now that sorta thing, well, in her family or in her town or in her church it just wouldn't fly.

We all carry the guilt of a suicide, and maybe because we couldn't go up there that night we felt guilty. But this wild party was not just a one-night thing, because it had been going on for days. Candy had been going to school every day and having this party at night. Nobody seemed to notice her having any problems at school.

Candy was looking to me for help that night, but she was also drunk enough that, if she was gonna do herself in, there was nothing much anybody or I could do. After all, I was three hundred miles away.

My mother thinks that, because I was the last sane person Candy talked to before she died, there was a part of Candy that stayed with me. I think that's ridiculous. I don't know, you probably don't really go into things like spiritual connections to the body in your work, but my mom wondered if there wasn't a kind of a spirit attachment.

Megan's mom explained:

I said that because, the last time Megan was home, about three weeks ago, we stayed up all night talking. We really needed to talk, because it seemed this was the only time we would be able to have this conversation. Megan brought some kids home with her from the city. It was one of these totally manic things and it was just like a crazy scene.

So that night, as she's talking to me, she started to get her cataplexy and her hypnagogic hallucinations, because you know Megan has narcolepsy. She had gone for twenty-four hours without her medication and she needed them. And she said, "Mom, I feel there's something in my throat that needs to get out."

So I just figured that she was already in an altered state, and I just started talking directly to whatever it was that was trying to express itself in her throat. And it was Candy, talking.

And so we talked to Candy, told her how much we love her and that she doesn't have to worry about us. What she has to do is follow her own path, and that she doesn't need to stay with Megan anymore. And that it's hampering Megan and that she needed to find and follow her own path. That she could leave.

So that's what we did. And it was so dramatic. And it was like at the end of this thing, so it was having a back-and-forth dialogue.

Megan clarified:

I felt Candy had passed, but my mom thought there still could be some residue. She says all this stuff about sometimes you don't get all of it. Sometimes there's more than one. Like sometimes there are nested entities. From different things. She says there may also be something from my childhood, but I don't know what it is.

In dysfunctional homes, kids in search of answers have a hard time finding them—or believing in the answers they do find. Unable to find what they're looking for, most give up on looking, but that road simply leads nowhere. Spirituality is a way for many to find answers on their own. It can open the doorway to philosophy, religion, psychology, and even therapy—which, in the best of instances, shines a light on the family and on the childhood pain, loss, and suffering that stem from problems at home.

I listened carefully to Megan's mom talk about spirituality, and I think she sensed some skepticism in my voice. "Now you may think that I'm all off with this spirit stuff," she said. She was right. I was a bit skeptical. Even so, my response was to take all of what she said with a grain of salt. I knew Megan, I had talked with her on a regular basis, and I'd heard it all before. It's not something that I thought Megan's mom was "off" about. Rather, I thought she was trying to find an explanation for her daughter's trauma, and this idea of spirit possession made sense to her. In the South, where I grew up, talk of voodoo, hoodoo, and spirit possession was commonplace in the church and in the community.

I told her I thought it was something she needed to pay attention to, and that I found it remarkable that she could talk about the whole matter with such calm matter-of-factness. I certainly didn't dismiss it. I know there are many things we cannot explain, and it seems Candy had led the kind of life where, even in death, there is no solace.

THE LAST STAND

David

David, at eighteen, wrote the following note:

Dear Mom:

I'm sorry I ended up such a big disappointment.

Love,

David

Lorrie was fourteen years old when her brother David committed suicide in the family garage. He was eighteen. Because he had grown up in a white, middle-class family, with all his apparent needs satisfied, his death was shocking to all, especially Lorrie. Sitting across from me, Lorrie removes the pen she has been holding sideways in her mouth and taps it on her leg. She's hesitant and visibly uneasy, obviously trying to find a way to talk about the most painful event in her life. As she presses through her nervous tapping, she begins to tell me her brother's death "had the most impact on me because I could see so much of him in me. David struggled to be liked, but was constantly rejected, and I think he felt hurt and misunderstood."

As I sat listening, watching her tears flow, I began to wonder whether I could face the sadness of teenage suicide with the same aloofness I had mustered with other ethnographic subjects I've studied.

The answer is obviously no, because this is different, if only because I think more about suicide than I have about other subjects, and I think often about the kids I know and what they might be thinking and doing. I also reflect on the issue because, often, what one kid feels and experiences, another kid feels the same way.

All this ran through my head as Lorrie, responding to my queries, tells me the circumstances of her brother's life. Once the conversation began, it was hard to stop, because this is a story about a family that will forever miss a part of itself, will always be reminded of that brother and son, every time a birthday comes around, a holiday drifts by, or a photograph stirs a memory.

Lorrie was a student in one of my classes who heard about my interest in teen suicide and decided to tell me about her brother. As with Megan's recounting of Candy's life in chapter 3, the process of understanding David's suicide through Lorrie's interpretation of his life is a kind of refracted narrative. David's life story is told through her. She is outlining what she perceives to be his trauma—David's broken familial relationships with his father and then his stepfather, and the attendant problems he had with his mother. Many of the stories I have been privy to have come through such a refracted prism.

David's story began in the early 1990s, in a suburban town with nice lawns and two-car garages. I begin David's story in the 1990s because I think it is important to map out a historical-cultural milieu, so that I can understand, at the very least, David's emotional inheritance and mind-set, the trends in social thought, music, and so forth that were contemporary to him. Although the commercialization and widespread use of the Internet did begin in the 1990s, this was before Facebook or other social media—

a source, today, of many clues about teenage disposition and feelings.

This kind of context is very important, but I believe that the emotional inheritance within the context of family life is multigenerational and that, therefore, to understand David's thinking —and the thinking of other teenagers discussed here—one really needs to understand more about his parents and grandparents, going backwards. It is, to a large degree, emotional archival work—a kind of mapping of unresolved issues that get passed down from one generation to another and that manifest themselves in various ways. I think the view is far more kaleidoscopic than photographic, in terms of ethnographic inquiry.

There is something else, too. I now understand that diaries and journal notes are distinct from what the public (through popular media) understands as a suicide note or parasuicide note(s), which is, really, what David's story is trying to convey. His suicide note reveals a totally defeated kid who feels not so much a need to punish others (although there is some element of that) as a clear desire to end the punishment, hurt, and sorrow he's felt all his life.

I did have many questions for Lorrie. For instance, did she have the actual and complete suicide note? Was it long? Short? Where was it found?

It is clear David wanted to please others, even while he suffers the ultimate fate. He wrote, "I'm sorry I ended up such a big disappointment." But he is also aware that he is not pleasing anyone, really, because his note is filled with irony. He knows everyone will suffer, now that he's dead, and that by his act he does something wrong to everybody.

Lorrie heard rumors that David's death might have been an accident. She is skeptical.

David hung himself in the garage, so it was very definitely not an accident. I mean, you don't accidentally hang yourself with your own shirt and leave a suicide note. I didn't live at home at that time; I was living in a different town when all of this happened.

My mom told me David had disappeared, and she was upset that he wasn't around, but I wasn't particularly worried because he had done this kinda thing before. He'd be missing, or hiding out somewhere, so this was not unusual. But what was unusual was this: we have a dog, and David was very close to it.

He'd taken the dog for a walk and had put it in the back yard. So the dog had been out all night. Well, the dog always slept inside. That was unusual, because although David was incredibly irresponsible, it was very strange that he would do something like that to the dog.

We don't know exactly when he did it; he hung up there for three or four days. You see, we don't use the garage to park our cars. My mom had reported him missing to the police after the third day.

I am not sure if, after three or four days, there would be a noticeable smell of decaying flesh, but I guess it would depend on the weather and if the body was in a cold or warm location.

On the fourth day, my mom discovered he hadn't picked up his paycheck. David had been working at Taco Bell. She figured that, if he were going to take off, he would have gone to pick up his paycheck. So that was kinda weird too.

After my mother called, I just figured he'd taken off without telling her. This was kind of on the strange side, but he'd done stranger things before, so although I remember having a bad feeling, I still went camping.

When I came back, I called my mom to see if she had any word about David, and when I heard her voice, I knew right away that he was either dead or in jail.

My mother tells me to talk to my father. Now, my parents are divorced, so why in the hell would my father be over there? So my dad gets on the phone. I already know my dad's a real good liar, because he's a cop. He lies for a living.

I ask him if David is dead. "No, no. Don't be ridiculous. Just come home right now. I need to talk to you immediately. I want my camping gear back."

I was like, *Oh yeah. Like there's a fucking camping emergency? Now you might as well just tell me he's dead, right?* But they were not gonna say it on the phone. They wanted to tell me in person.

When Lorrie arrived home, the yard was full of cars and, inside, family friends and neighbors were cleaning up. Unusual activity. Something was definitely wrong.

My mom has told me that David was a highly sensitive child. He was very much doted on, because he was the youngest boy for a couple of years. He was very angelic—blond hair, chubby cheeks. And he looked small for his age, so you could see how he would be treated like a baby all the time.

My older sister can remember always walking him to school when he was little. He would never walk to school by himself, even when he was old enough. He would wait after school for her, even if his classes got out earlier, to be walked back home. And the distance between the elementary school and my house is like three blocks. When my parents got married [Lorrie and David have different fathers], I think David would have been maybe five years old. He didn't have much of a relationship with his father. I've met his dad on more than one occasion, and I liked the man. He didn't come off as cruel or vindictive, but I can't say he was really around much for his kids, either. I think the best that could be said of him is he probably did the most with what he had to work with at the time. And he eventually got remarried and started a new family.

When our mom married my dad, David would have been three or four. After she divorced David's dad and married my dad, David immediately latched on to my dad. He was close to my dad up until the very end. I think my dad was the only person he ever trusted. He harbored such a complete hatred for our mom; I mean, it was abnormal. He definitely held her responsible for the divorces from his father and then, later, from my father.

I think all of us held my mom responsible for divorcing our dads. She's a recovering alcoholic, an incredibly flighty and nervous Valium-popping, martini-swigging, Donna Karan–dressing kind of high-pumped woman who was, like, always on and off the wagon.

David and I fought a lot, I think, because of that kind of dynamic where I'm spoiled and he's older by a few years. We ended up being close, I think more than anything else, because we spent the longest amount of time living together.

I remember that David's adolescence was horrible because our mom and my dad got divorced around that time. It was devastating for David. He didn't have a lot of friends. He had his best friend, Grant, who lived up the street from us, that he sort of followed around. But that was kind of it. I mean, there was negative interest for David toward both girls and boys. He did get in trouble a couple of times for calling sex party lines, so he must have had some kind of sexual impulse.

But this process of detaching himself from everybody started early, and I remember him more angry and detached as he hit his midteens. He really had a negative interest even in himself, in how he looked. I can remember how disheveled he was as a child and as a teenager.

As David got older, I noticed how he withdrew into himself, until he began to experiment with drugs. He continually got in trouble. He wasn't a real bright kid; he'd get in trouble for really stupid things. Like he would borrow my mom's car and then leave a bag of weed on the passenger seat.

I asked Lorrie what she thought that meant. I can tell this is wearing on her. I ask if she wants to stop. She says nothing for a moment, holds her head down, then raises her hands to her face to indicate her readiness to continue. As she talks, a pained expression fills her face again and, at the same moment, a vein streaks across her brow. It is a look that belongs to the real story of her past and the details of the life of a lost brother.

When David was older, late teens, my mom would try to kick him out of the house. He would sleep with a sleeping bag in his car, and I would be crying, telling Mom to let him back inside. I couldn't stand it. It was so upsetting and ridiculous. I would look at him and think, *How horrible. My brother's homeless.* Finally, she would let him in.

He would yell and scream. It was the only way he could communicate with my mom. Sometimes, he would scream out, "Mom, you make me fucking crazy." Which I think was his way of saying, "You are the reason I'm like this." And my mom certainly did her share of fucking up the kids' heads pretty soundly.

I don't know if she meant to fuck him up in a conscious way, but it all boils down to the same thing. She had alcohol and drug problems, and the kids she had from her first marriage went through two divorces—really nasty divorces. All of this had very negative effects.

I asked Lorrie to talk about the happy moments she and her family shared with David. I wondered if she would recall the last time they laughed together. She produced some photographs.

This is the last Christmas [and the last time] I saw him. We both look very happy, but I don't think he really was.

David was very unhappy after that last Christmas we spent together. I was concerned about him that day. Very concerned. He killed himself later that year. I just remember thinking if I were David, I would hate my life too. And the reason I would hate my life? I would not want to be an aging kid, flipping burgers, going nowhere, while my classmates rode around in their cars; living with my mom in that same fucking house, where every horrible thing I could remember happened. Every fight he'd ever seen my parents have had taken place in that house. He probably lost count how many times he'd seen my mom get drunk and fall on the stairs.

Lorrie had a premonition:

At the time, I had just come down from the mountains. I had a feeling something was wrong right away. I can remember going into the kitchen and saying, really demanding, "OK. Is he dead?" Because I remember just wanting to know. I remember feeling very fucked with! Dad lied on the phone about the whole thing.

There were people all over the house, vacuuming, cleaning. Neighbors making coffee and stuff. What the fuck was that all about? And I didn't see David.

I asked my dad what had happened and he said, "Wait." Then I knew something was really wrong.

My godmother was there, and then my dad said, "Wait for your mom, wait for your mom. We're gonna do this as a family." And I remember thinking, *Oh, fuck.* 'Cause you don't hear that "family" bit very often at my house.

My mom came down the stairs, and I took one look at her and thought, *Oh, shit. She is never ever gonna be the same again.* I remember just knowing that, and I was right. To this day, it's like a little part of her is dead. It's like someone took a little piece of that woman and just . . . kind of squished it out.

My dad got on his professional look, and I remember he took my hand and said, "Lorrie, David's dead." And I just said, "Why did he do it?" 'Cause I knew. And he said, "We don't know, but he hung himself in the garage."

I was really hoping that he had done it outside. Somewhere out of the house. I knew that if he had done it at home, my mom would've had to have found him. I remember thinking, right then, that if I had ever believed in God, this was the time I lost that belief. I did not believe in God anymore. Because if there was a God, he would not have let my brother hang there for three days and then let my mother find him.

I thought it was very odd that he was dead for three days and my mom couldn't find him. Apparently, my other brother asked her if she'd checked the garage. She said that she'd opened the door and looked around the garage and hadn't seen anything. None of us can explain that, except that maybe she did see something and just refused to see it. It is possible she could have dismissed any odors as well.

I don't know if anyone was in the house during that time, and by the time they found him, he must have been reeking awfully at that point. She may have looked for him before the odor set in.

According to the coroner, he definitely would have been there when she looked, because that was the day before he was found. And then, I guess, she talked to my brother again and he said, "Did you check everywhere in the house?" And she went back to the garage, looked again, and she saw him.

My mom and dad spent a lotta time entertaining and pleasing people—everybody but us. My brother and me were not what they cared about. That's why he's dead now. I blame them. I don't think they had his best interests in mind. I think they just thought if they bought him things, that would be enough.

Lorrie's mother wanted David to have a Catholic funeral.

We could not believe Mom decided to have a Catholic funeral, because it was the absolute last thing David would have wanted. But if it's gonna make Mom feel better, you know, let her do it.

There was a wake, and then there was an actual Catholic service, which is hard to arrange because, you know, Catholics aren't real fond of the whole suicide situation. But my mother's name is Demarco, and you don't screw with a person that Catholic. She insisted.

So they had a Catholic Mass, and they had another little Mass by the burial site, the whole deal, which David would have absolutely fucking hated. It's so ironic. Knowing David, he would have just wanted to be cremated and thrown into the sea or something.

The grief experienced by a suicide victim's family can take unusual forms. Lorrie relates what happened to her mother after David's death.

My mother took the whole thing very hard and had some rather bizarre reactions. One day, well after the suicide, I was visiting home, in my room with my dog. The dog gets up, goes out, and comes back with this plastic bag that smells like shit. I got up to see what she had, and all of a sudden the smell is worse.

I'm used to the dog finding weird things, but I'm thinking, *What the hell's she dug up now?* The dog's got the plastic bag, rips it open, and inside is David's jeans and underwear.

The dog got the bag from my mother's closet. David's clothes, the clothes that he killed himself in, had been in her closet all this time. After she got them from the coroner, she kept them in her closet with her own clothes. The shit that I smelled was the underwear that he died in, 'cause you shit when you hang yourself. I thought, *Fuck! My mother has gone absolutely crazy!* I said, "Mom! You can't keep the shorts he shitted in when he died, in the fucking closet. You can't do it. This is just not healthy." She was kind of like, "Yeah, I guess you're right."

I don't know what she did with them after that, but I was like, "I can't have you living like this." I thought this was it, but not long after that, I came home to visit and found out she has been sleeping with the suicide note in her bed.

When you have a wake, you make a memorial board with photos—like, David as a baby and all that kind of stuff. And she's got the board in her room. She has decided to live with it around her. She's also taken to being like David in some ways. Reclusive. She stays in bed, has dishes all over the floor. The place is a mess.

This is a woman who never did this kind of shit before. Now I'm wondering when I'm gonna find my mom hanging in the garage.

My mom's behavior was very bizarre, but I think she was just so harmed by David's death—and perhaps felt guilty about all the things that went on with her and him—that she never got over it. Since all this happened, I can't be close to my Mom, because I used to really rely on her a lot, really confide in her about my problems. I can't do that now, because she's pretty destroyed. I don't know if she's ever gonna fully recover from this.

The grief of David's mother brings to mind the mother of a slain teenager, depicted in Elijah Anderson's *Code of the Street*, who was so grief-stricken that she wore her son's basketball jersey while walking the streets of Philadelphia.[1]

Lorrie says:

I often think about why David killed himself, and I can't recall any particular, solitary event that happened. I think there were a lot of little things. There were continuous little tries that he would make, and then fail. And he would always end up returning home.

David didn't really write things. The suicide note would have been easy to find, because he never wrote anything. To find anything with his handwriting on it would have been amazing. He never had any outward form of expression. There was no drawing, no writing. Nothing.

When David hung himself, he was facing away from the house. I know he was trying to get out, one way or the other. I just don't think he felt there was a place for him in the family.

Lorrie says David never wrote anything, as far as she knows. But suppose he did and she was not able to find it? It is possible he did write more than she supposes. At any rate, he did write the suicide note, and he made it easy to find. David's narrative is markedly different from that of the teens profiled here who committed suicide, including Candy's narrative (chapter 3), in that he did not leave a trail of parasuicidal notes before his suicide and did not belong to a network of shared feelings with other teenagers his age. He seems to have been a loner, and very aloof.

Of course, the main question is why Lorrie did not provide the note in its entirety. When Lorrie was asked about this, she said that this was all he wrote.

David, like Kyra (chapter 1), experienced a core trauma. Kyra's father died when she was three years old; David lost his father, and then his stepfather, through divorce. In each case, this becomes a core trauma.

For Lorrie the memory of what happened to her brother is the one reason she says:

> I can't stand that house. I couldn't stand it before my brother killed himself and I can't stand it now. We always had enough money. We always had that kind of shit. But that is not an emotionally easy place to live. Sometimes you need more than money.

5

HOMO

Tucker

Tucker, a teenage boy lives at home and wrote this diary note:

> To my parents: Fuck you. I don't care. You'll be the one who did it to me. I can kill myself if I want. You have no control over me.

Tucker is a short, skinny, white kid with a startled look on his round, puffy face. He sits across from me, with his friends, speaking quietly and resolutely, his voice a low monotone raised just above a whisper as he talks about his life, parents, and friends. In spite of this reticence, he has a sharp though unassuming wit, and deep penetrating eyes.

At first glance, his eyes jump out at you like he's surprised to see you—as a child might look when he sees his mother coming and rushes out to greet her. The baggy pants and old sweatshirt make him look even smaller, and an unlaced pair of well-worn sneakers peeks out from under the ragged-edged cuffs. Tucker is a thinker, and at any given time you will notice he's deep in thought, his head down, pulling his chin, twirling his hair in a constant ritual.

He and I begin talking about his homosexuality and end with a discussion about his parents. He insists his parents knew nothing about him being gay until he told them after high school. He'd tried to tell them many times but had lost the nerve, and when he attempted to tell them through his actions they didn't seem to get it. He tells of a time he invited his boyfriend over and they stayed in the summer cottage together, spending almost the entire time there without communicating with his parents, emerging one morning after a wild night of sex, holding hands, only to break up the touching as they entered the main house where his parents were staying.

I ask Tucker what his home life is like.

Why do you ask that? Is it because of my obsession with suicide? I don't know everything that caused me to react to stuff all the time. Or at least, I don't think I know. But on the other hand I think I do know. I know I was depressed as a kid because my dad always wanted me to be what I didn't want to be. He used to badger me, from as long as I can remember, to be a baseball player, be a football player, be this, be that. But I didn't play baseball or basketball or any of those things, but he insisted. So by the time I got to be seven or eight I had been depressed for four years already. You see, my dad was into this macho thing that in order to be a man you had to be a jock or you had to be successful and make money. There was no in-between. You couldn't be anything unless it was what he wanted you to be.

In his diary, Tucker wrote:

Dear diary;

Today I felt so drained like all the life in me is being sucked completely out. Thoughts of suicide that haven't entered my mind since a while ago are constantly flowing through my mind. It's like I can't figure out the meaning of life questions about suicide . . . suicide keeps coming in my mind like how, why, and would I really ever do it? The thought of death confuses me but in a way it scares me and excites me. Is it that stupid? I just wish there was someone to talk to but guidance counselors and parents don't fit the bill. Why did I have to be different from everyone else?

Tucker tells me:

My parents were not interested in my sex life, nor did they think I ever had one to start with. They were very religious, and I think, had they knew while I was home that I may have been having sex with boys, they would have just died. Anyway, we never discussed homosexuality or anything like that because it was a totally taboo subject.

After I came out with them, I was leaving for college, and after that they just said, "It's your life. You have to live it the way you please." That was my mom. My dad just stood there for a moment, looking very uncomfortable and sad-faced. Finally, he just said, "Yeah. Your mother is right it's your life."

So after a few more awkward moments I left and went to my room. I was both relieved and a bit sad at that time. I sat in my room for a long time and just looked out the window. Looking out into the world, feeling free and disgusted, but more free than disgusted as the hour slipped by. I heard my mother calling me and I snapped out of it because they both wanted to take me to the train station.

My stuff was all packed, and when I got downstairs my dad said he'd say good-bye now because my mom would drive me. Now, he'd always driven me at times like this—you know, to camp, or that time I went on the upstate trip—and we'd talk sports the whole way and whatnot. But not this time, and I knew why. I just went over and shook his hand and I was off.

The next time I saw my dad was when I came home for the holidays, and he seemed a little better, but he made a comment at the dinner table, about never having grandchildren, that kinda put an edge on the whole affair. I didn't say anything, and my sister just looked at me. It was as if he wasn't talking to her, just me, but I let it go and finished eating. I talked to him later and I told him nothing is impossible, and he looked at me with the most curious look and tilted his head a bit and said, "Yeah, Tuck, nothing is impossible."

You see, this is typical of my dad. Not so much my mother, because I could talk to her. She was okay with my lifestyle and told me she loved me no matter what and we'd talk about these things, but dad never would say anything beyond the surface.

We never got to the depth of a thing, and my guess is he was worried about being the scapegoat—you know, the macho man feeling he's the weakest link. As if my being gay was his fault. Maybe he was worried about what our conversations might reveal about him. I don't know exactly what it was, but I do know he chose not to talk to me in any way that may have shed light on how he really felt, or in any way that made me feel comfortable with myself. Maybe he just wanted me to suffer. I don't know.

Tucker started cutting himself in junior high school because it was the thing to do. Cutting or self-harm can be as popular a sport among some kids as basketball and soccer is among others. It's cool, or it may be for self-satisfaction, a stress-releasing addiction, punishing oneself, or some kind of masturbation. Typically, they know the self-infliction will not bring death, but the cuts do act as "pain notches," and they use the scars to express pride in their suffering. For Tucker, to cut is to feel, and to feel is to be alive. Cutting or self-mutilation is one of the recurring characteristics of the teenagers depicted in this book, and Tucker is no exception. He tells me:

I started cutting around thirteen or fourteen, and it was the first time I used a knife on myself. I talked myself into doing it. I told my parents so many times that I was gonna kill myself that afterwards they were fuckin' scared outta their minds. But in my freshman year they found some coke in my room and were so upset with me that I was the one scared then. They kept me grounded for weeks after that. But this just caused me to be so much more angry with them.

I had all this rage inside of me, because I had already felt that my room was like my cell, and having to stay there when I didn't really want to caused even more rage within me. So I started cutting myself to release some of this tension and rage inside. It made me let go.

In his diary, Tucker described some of the self-harm and associated feelings:

I peeled off my chest and screamed out as my eyes sunk deep into my skull. My feminine fingernails are tools to my distraction
I loved it. I pressed my glowing cigarette into my arm.
I shut up when my mom walked into the room once again. She didn't knock, she never does.

In trying to limit his self-mutilation to cutting, Tucker quickly discovered that the deeper he cut, the more intense was the "feeling."

I had this real mean scar to show how deep I felt the need to let all of this tension go. The release was not about the blood. I know a lot of kids are into the blood-ritual stuff, but for me it was the feeling, sorta like a massage type thing. I took dull scissors and ran it across my arms and legs. I never really drew blood most of the time. It would press into the skin. The release is like you haven't cried in a long time and one day you finally do cry, and then you get hysterical and can't stop, and when you do, you feel relieved. Your body and mind feel free and you feel better.

One day my mother saw this scar, and it totally fucked her up. She was freaking out. I had a bad scar, but it wasn't like my body was all cut up. She started saying that I had to go see a psychiatrist and all of that.

For the most part, Tucker's parents grew increasingly frustrated with his antics, and their actions fluctuated from sheer open-mouthed fright/shock to believing it was some kind of boy-who-cried-wolf syndrome, in which they simply didn't believe he would do anything.

My parents essentially said, after a while, that if I was gonna kill myself, "Go ahead. Let's see." I think my mother was always a little bit hurt by my saying I was gonna kill myself, but my dad just got angry at me for putting them through so much.

I had an intense preoccupation with suicide when I was a kid. I started thinking about suicide in the second grade, probably seven or eight years old. I remember my teacher had us read these small novels about dying, and one story was about a little boy who drowned in a river near his house. I'm not sure why I put dying and suicide together but I did, although my teacher was trying to get us to understand grieving at a young age.

I do know that around that time my grandfather died, and those two things—the novels [Dostoyevsky, *Anna Karenina*, and W. Somerset Maugham's *The Moon and Sixpence*] and his death—got me obsessed with death. There were other things going on in my life, too, that caused me to think about death and dying. First of all, I was the youngest in my family and needed more attention from my parents than I got, mostly because, at that time, my sister was in her last year of high school and was acting out and my parents were dealing with her.

My sister was giving my parents fits because she was smoking pot, staying out late, and not doing all that well in school. I was left alone. I thought one of the ways I could get back at them was to commit suicide. Suicide became my way out. It was my way of making a big statement. I was also trying to understand what my sexuality was all about, too.

My friends were going through some of the same things around understanding about sex and stuff. And so I was just trying to present myself in a certain way. But I knew—given my sixteen-year-since perspective on all of this—I was trying to present—no, I was presenting—a false reality, because I had different feelings than I was presenting, both on the outside, to my friends, and on the inside, to my family. So I began to value my life alone. I was alone a lot more. I mean, I would lock myself in my room and stay in there. It was my cell.

I was trying to deal with my thoughts and everything that bothered me, and suicide became this very easy way out. I wanted to live this very intense life because I was hiding so much. And so suicide became this big secret.

Suicide, as Tucker saw it, was a no-win situation. The hiding and the suicide became his escape route. He, like other kids his age, had no conception of what it's like to be without their parents, and some, like Tucker, felt trapped by those parents. "I felt this hold my parents had on me and thought it would never end. And the only way I could see to get out of that hold was to kill myself."

Tucker removes a piece of crumpled paper from his backpack and reads a poem he's written.

> Imagine nothing. I'm in pain.
> I am captive.
> I am held in four walls.
> A hell by my own imagination.

I was a pretty severely depressed kid from about eight years old. I was in this place that was so hard and so different from where other kids were. Looking into myself, at myself, mortality and time and the power of nature. I was trying to break down things like religion. I used to see a psychologist for depression, and the whole obsession I had with suicide made me sure I would be dead by the time I hit my teens.

I was not a model kid growing up in a small town. I was a lot of trouble for my parents. But I taught them a lot about tolerance.

Some parents can't wait to relinquish their responsibility for their kids. They forget they are responsible for a much longer period than previous generations. In America, we believe the responsibility for our children ends after eighteen years, because parents really want that obligation lifted from their shoulders at a specific time. Most of the kids I talked to felt that parental obligations, nurturing, and support should continue well beyond those years. But it is clear, too, that there was an abdication of parental responsibility long before Tucker reached eighteen years of age, and very little empathy for the complicated feelings of teenagers, such as growing pains, confusion, and angst. Thus, this case is also a meditation, if you will, on what being a parent means, more than anything else. And, of course, this is also deeply complicated by gender, religious beliefs, and emotional inheritance over the course of several generations.

But at the same time there are businesspeople parents, single fathers and mothers, or drug-addicted families who are too busy or too drugged or otherwise unprepared as parents to meet the demands of parenting, even when their kids are five or six years old.

Tucker developed an interest in cameras, photography, and video recordings at age twelve. Recognizing this interest, his parents bought him a video camera for his thirteenth birthday. Tucker, in the throes of depression and anger, uncertain about his sexuality, continued to fixate on suicide while he played with his new technology toys.

> I got my own video camera and recorded my suicide note on videotape. I felt I would die either environmentally, naturally, or I would be killing myself by my own hands. So, at thirteen my suicidal thoughts and writing continued, and so did my desire to die.

Tucker felt the need to get back at his parents, not so much for what they did to him but for what they did not do—that is, because they did not probe enough to find out why he spent so much time in his room feeling worthless, lonely, and isolated. He said he'd commit suicide by overdosing on drugs. "I thought, since they never come to my room, I'd just do every drug I could find and just die in my room. They would find me a week later or something like that."

Although overdosing more than once, whether intentional or not, is sometimes a precursor to suicide, it is definitely always an indication that something is seriously wrong, which is why it absolutely needs to be dealt with right away.

Tucker wrote:

And I got this friggin book (diary) when I was 12 years old—and now, tonight I lay in my bed as a seventeen years old. But I am done. I have been—although not engulfed in depression I am no longer valuing life—I am tired and finished. Kat Pos, Lena, Candy, Erika Blough, that freshman girl, Danita Gilmanan's entire family, death. My prophecy came and strangled life out of these humans and so? Why not me? I am ready. I am beyond this my death my nudity, today I have tried twice and a sex and love and I be alone forever? I am done.

Tucker explains:

So why did I think of suicide at that age? Well, the thing with the novels about death and my grandfather dying was just a trigger I guess. It was just a thing I got my head wrapped around, because it was after that I was going to church with my mother all the time and my dad never really went. It was me and my mom, and I became very religious and felt the way to get relief was to be religious and believe in God, and I did. I think I became obsessed with Jesus as an icon. And by the time I was twelve I was sure I could be with Jesus by dying for other people's sins. The sins of my father, for not understanding me, for not letting me be who I wanted to be.

Tucker joined a group called Yashua ("Jesus Freaks," to his friends). He was an easy recruit because he was eager to get close to men, and when he was approached by a young male adherent he immediately developed an attachment.

The guys all look like hippies, and I looked like them in the way I dressed and everything, and I didn't look my age. The guys all have long ponytails. It's actually a one-fist ponytail and it symbolizes control.

I lost my dad when we couldn't communicate any longer, so I wanted to have a closer relationship with a man.

I think he (the Yashua recruiter) was the first male I felt some twang of feeling for (besides my dad), and he invited me to dinner, which is their approach to convert kids. A lot of kids are invited to dinner, and that's where they tell you how they work. They have home teaching instead of regular school. And the man is the dominant force in the family and all the women have to be obedient to the man. A lot of the girls don't like that and so it's harder to recruit girls.

Basically, my dad didn't accept me for who I was. Bottom line. He felt I should be only what he wanted. I had two sisters and was the only male. The last in the line. I had to meet his expectations, and that was that. I was under that pressure from a little boy, and it drove me nuts.

Tucker's father stood over him, asking questions about baseball statistics, asking him to recite what players made how many points in this game or the other, and that sort of thing. Tucker recalls:

I remember being outside my body and watching this little boy try to come up with all the right numbers for my father, who is pushing me to get the numbers right and drilling this into my head. And he'd slap me on the back, saying, "You remember, it was Green Bay, 1968. You know this stuff—28 to 16 over Baltimore," or something like that. It was awful.

It was awful because Tucker wasn't really interested in sports or statistics and would have preferred to watch a movie or make art with his sisters.

His father's rather overbearing approach and high expectations forced Tucker into a role as the father's "boy wonder," who was to become a great football player and a success at whatever he happened to do in life. But when Tucker expressed misgivings, his father berated him and made him feel weak, and because Tucker wanted to please his father, this burden became overwhelming.

I hated my father for his pushing me so much, and I remember writing "Father is death 2 life" on my hand one time, after he told me I should stop talking about all this suicide stuff and focus on living and learning and doing better in school.

My mother was on his side most of the time, especially when it came to pushing me to succeed, and no matter what grades I made, it was never good enough.

Tucker felt a real burden to prove to himself—but especially to prove to his father—that he could be what his father wanted. But, as the years went by, Tucker felt more and more that he was living a lie. He had no way to weigh all of that at the time, at five or six years old, and it manifested itself in his obsession with ending it all, with suicide and the belief in sacrificing himself. He wrote:

Father you don't realize your own actions, I say you mean nothing and although I was correct, you know how to fuck me over the

best out of anyone I have ever met . . . You don't approve of me.
I don't approve of you. This is all true. My blood will never be on
your hands. You'd never bother to clean it up. You're already dead.

Tucker looked for jobs around town but had a few prospects.
As summer arrived, he noticed that his father was in a sunnier
mood, though something told him it was not to last.

One summer I was sitting at the table and my father comes in and
says he has a present for me. And he takes me outside, and he'd
bought me a car. This was great. So I told him I had a surprise for
him, and that I had a job delivering pizza and the car would be a
great help. Instead of him being proud of me for getting a job, he
puts me down by saying I should have gotten a better job with
some substance and that I shouldn't be driving the car around delivering pizza.

I think my dad is really ridiculous when he's being critical like
that.

All right, he wants me to be successful. That's fine. But why
hark on it and hark on it [*sic*] to the point where I'm so resentful
that I can't even think straight and begin to hate him for it?

And my mom, who I love to death, never really challenged all
of that at first. But later she did, and wanted me to be successful,
too, but without the pressure. She would say, "Be who and what
you want to be." She supported me, after a while.

Tucker thought something was wrong with him, and he felt
he was somehow different, but what kept him from committing
suicide, or taking those "suicidal moments" to their final hour, remained a puzzle. He wanted to blame his parents, but he knew
they couldn't take the blame if he wasn't sure of his problem.

He was, however, using his suicidal moments to threaten his parents.

The only certainty Tucker felt about life at that time was his "date with death," fixed at sixteen, because he knew that if he had not released what he was feeling by then, he'd explode.

A leading psychotherapist, Dr. Susan Kornblum, told me, "Gay teenagers are more likely to commit suicide because they often feel the need to conceal their sexuality, and when they do that they begin to feel isolated, alienated from friends and family. But you must remember, despite these feelings, they all give warning signs when they are thinking about committing suicide."

The warning signs for Tucker's parents should have been obvious, because he expressed his feelings loudly, as most teens contemplating suicide do—in dress, actions, sending out glaring signals. These warning signs are not limited to gay and lesbian teens but extend to all suicidal youths. The signs include writing, threats, expressing feelings of death, or making casual jokes about killing oneself. In some cases, a sure indication that something may be wrong is that a young person begins giving away valuable possessions, consuming unhealthy amounts of drugs, or is overly depressed for some time and then is suddenly cheerful. Many kids who decide to commit suicide become happy because they've made a decision to end their life, and the depression is lifted because this very big problem has been finally solved. But Tucker had not reached that point of bliss yet.

I said that, by the time I was in seventh or eighth grade, at first, would be the time. And I was sure sixteen was the year I was gonna die. I felt that if twelve to sixteen was the apex of your life—then I would rather be living really intensely until then.

Things were working out fine, because—around thirteen, when my sister was smoking pot and acting out and being the badass in the family—my parents didn't notice me so much, and they concentrated solely on her. But when she left the house and they found I had similar problems, experimenting with drugs and stuff like that, we started having arguments. That's when I started threatening them with talk about suicide.

While Tucker constantly screamed suicide, his parents grew more and more frustrated at his "fake" attempts, until they felt their son needed spiritual guidance, as one possible solution. Tucker was calling for help each time he locked himself in his room, smoked a joint, or made a threat. He was reaching out to his parents to do something, anything—to pay attention to him, talk to him, or call someone who might listen.

I think my dad had no clue about what might be bothering me or where this was coming from, because he had no idea of this kinda stuff when he was a kid. And he would say, "Why do you have to be so fucked up? You know if you kill yourself the world won't end."

My dad was Catholic, and since I was also trying to understand religion at that time, he would always tell us that religion was something inside you. So I understood religion to be the spirituality inside of you. By that logic, if I killed myself, since I'm the center of my world, then the world is over for me.

So it seemed completely ridiculous and mean for my dad to keep saying that, because on the one hand he was saying that the world would go on without me, and on the other that he didn't care what I did. Meanwhile, I keep feeling that there was nothing I could do. I felt completely helpless. But I kept thinking what could solve this miserable depression, because no matter what happened, I knew the end would come at sixteen, when I'd kill myself. So I just started counting the years.

I also knew why I became obsessed with killing myself, because I just kept rationalizing everything. I knew that every young kid knew someone who had died. And no one close to me had died. So I thought maybe I was that person who had to die for everyone else. So I became obsessed with that kind of thought process until my junior year of high school.

I do believe kids like Tucker reach a point in their suicidal process at which they begin to rationalize what they are about to do, and I believe Tucker had several underlying issues to contend with, issues that had not surfaced, all of which contributed to his ordeal. The first and foremost issue was his closeted gay life, about which he said nothing to anyone, because he felt no one would be sympathetic.

During that time, I felt like I was the only gay kid in the world. I would sit in my room and remember the times when I would crawl up in my father's arms and feel so comfortable, so safe there. I wondered if that was why I started to like older men.

This last comment brought a slight smile to his face, a look he doesn't show all that often. But wanting to end his life became an obsession, because it seemed his only way out of the misery he no longer wanted to endure. Then, something changed.

Then I lost two friends to suicide in high school. They killed themselves over boredom, fucked-up parents, parental neglect, drugs, depression, drugs, whatever, and I felt they must be replacing me. So I vowed I would not kill myself after that, and I made it through my sixteenth year and started to dress differently, hang out with "good kids," and in general change my whole perspective. I started seeing girls, doing well in school. My parents were happy with my schoolwork. I was really trying hard at that time to change a lot of what I had been doing so negatively.

There is little doubt that the loss of his friends to suicide became a cathartic antisuicide moment for Tucker, because at that point he began to see how much he wanted to live and make a difference in the lives of gay kids.

I was still smoking pot every few days, because it was my one soft moment. I had moved from smoking just on weekends. It was my one relaxing time, when I could laugh and just be myself. It was one of those things that made me happy, but only for a short time.

In the absence of parents or peers who can help teenagers better cope with the realities of growing up, kids often turn to drugs, alcohol, or alternate means of stimulation to dull themselves from the pain and confusion of life. But continued drug and alcohol misuse only exacerbates the deep-rooted issues. Dulling the mind creates an alternate reality that prevents any real growth or learning. These highs, which last for only a short time, are quickly followed by an even deeper depression, and the cycle of misuse continues to repeat itself as the internal problems of the teenager continue to simmer and get worse.

Most of the time I was depressed, every day, all day long, and my body image was all fucked up. My body was disgusting, but when

I got high at night with my friends, just laugh or just enjoy music, it seemed like my serotonin level would just rise and I could forget all about those things. So you'd think smoking was good for me because I'd at least have this normal serotonin level on a daily basis.

Serotonin is a neurotransmitter commonly believed to contribute to feelings of happiness. So Tucker saw marijuana as therapeutic, as do other kids who try to fix themselves by using drugs and alcohol, and writing cures, and talking out with friends. He used the pot as a way to deal with the anxiety caused by his parents, his loneliness, and his closeted gay secret. But he also began another coping method, self-mutilation, to release the tension in his body and his head. He was gaining weight, saw himself as chubby and too short, developed acne, and began fantasizing about men and boys obsessively.

While Tucker saw his marijuana and cocaine use as therapeutic, his parents were alarmed because of what they knew about the dangers of the drug, and they sought to punish him for it. Tucker, however, rationalized that he was not harming anyone but himself, which is exactly what he wanted to do. Again, this was a warning sign from him to them, a cry for help, but because of this ongoing kid–parent power-sharing dynamic, help was not part of the formula and was lost in the cycle.

I didn't think I'd make it as far as sixteen, so when I turned seventeen I knew I had made it to a point in my life where things had to change. I had to change. I had just stopped cutting myself and was moving into more positive things. Of course I was still suppressing my sexuality but that was a problem I knew I had to deal with eventually.

Tucker thought of ways to deal with his sexuality but was still conflicted.

And I hid from myself inside this boy . . . coming out today
And it can only be said in screams—aloud—I scream
Violence, and my hours slashed by these voices
Melting chains—set I free—but I will not stay dumb.

Tucker continued to reflect on the matter, and for a moment, he thought he would talk with his father. Kids feel they should be able to talk about anything with their parents, but this is rarely the case, especially when the subject is sex or death/suicide. These two areas remain largely taboo.

The experience among many of the kids I have encountered suggests that coming to terms with being gay or lesbian has an even deeper impact on their lives than other problems at home or school. These kids are dealing with complicated and lasting questions about who they are. Is this normal? Who should I tell? Am I alone? The answer is that it's completely normal, they are not alone, and speaking out to a trusted friend, counselor, or select family member can help them realize this fact and begin the process of understanding and acceptance that will allow them to embrace and celebrate who they are.

Most kids' first role model for open discussion of taboo subjects, or for any kind of meaningful discussion, is one or both parents. But kids only attempt such taboo talk once or twice, and if parents are not open, the kids usually won't mention it again. Because conversations about sex and death are avoided or are openly mentioned only rarely, most kids see these topics as not worthy of discussion, as "bad" talk that should be hidden. Therefore, it is helpful if parents can be more aware of their kids when a sensitive subject comes up. And if a kid is not ready to discuss at that particular moment, parents should try to make a point of seriously addressing the subject at a later time. Otherwise, the moment is lost, because kids will not want to be rejected again.

> Parents are never freed from the burden of their children. If you have kids, you are a parent until you die. The only thing you should be concerned about is being a parent. It does not mean that you can't pursue your own interest and hobbies, but you are first and foremost a parent, and your life should revolve around your children.

I expect a more thorough analysis would include a look at how parenting skills, and in some cases, parenting expectations, impacted by ethnicity, class, sexuality, religion, or race, would perhaps apply here, to explain how these variables relate what is happening in this book, but perhaps this is beyond the scope of the work.

From the perspective of three-dimensional ethnography (the attempt to understand a place or informant beyond his or her own narrative), I think the key here is to understand the parenting process, and the history of a child, as an emotional inheritance over generations. To some degree, that is what a parent is. Interviews with the parents of these teenagers would have added a dynamic understanding of the relationship between their parenting style and their own childhood histories, but opportunities for such interviews did not present themselves. A key question is to examine the psychotherapeutic literature and see what it has to say about treating a "family" within the context of teen parasuicide/suicide.

Tucker's lack of direct communication with his parents about taboo subjects forced him to get information from books, and mostly from friends. He provided subtle and not so subtle hints—to his father on occasion, to his mother more often—about his "secret," but neither parent responded. Such clues included closeting himself in his room, sleeping excessively, refusing to talk, missing school, lying, smoking cigarettes and marijuana, and using other chemicals.

The more obvious signs available to parents are drug paraphernalia left around, cuts on the body, overly secretive behavior, spending long hours away from home, or having friends outside of one's peer group. When parents do see behavior they find alarming, they may scream, physically attack, or react so negatively that children only continue this behavior to an increasing degree.

> I thought I was gay around ten years old, because that's when I began masturbating to men. By the time I was thirteen, I knew it. I began to say that to myself: *I'm gay? But what does that mean, being gay?*

Tucker's story seems similar to that of Candy (chapter 3), who was struggling with her bisexual or possibly lesbian identity.

> But I couldn't ask anyone else. I had to keep it to myself. And all of that led me to keep trying to pull off the illusion that I was "normal." I would play boy sports, soccer and stuff like that. This was around seventh grade; this was right when my sister was giving my parents trouble, so they were ignoring me.

But Tucker suddenly stopped pretending to like sports, didn't spend Saturday talking sports with his father, and stopped wear-

ing "nice" clothes and befriending "good, neat kids" on the block.
The change was as inexplicable to his parents as it was to teachers
and others around him. It was the beginning of his coming out.

I started to make a drastic change in my behavior, because I
stopped hanging out with the kids who were into sports and wearing nice, ironed shirts and creased pants and stuff. I started wearing grunge, real funky gear, and then I started hanging out more
with the kids on the fringe. I guess you could say that the grunge,
funky gear, fringe are signifiers and signs of alienation.

These were the kids who were depressed but had no way to
express what we were feeling. That's when I started smoking pot
every day, trying to deal with both my suicide fixation and my being gay. These two things were driving me crazy.

Just as Tucker thought he'd put suicide behind him and decided to "help other gay kids," he fell into a funk, a glaring con-
flated hostility. He wanted to scream.

I can no longer contain myself inside these walls
You fucking faggot, you fucking faggot, you faggot—and my
sight becomes blurred as I stare into his eyes—beautiful sin
I touch my lips—so gently to your cheek and employ my
tongue—pressing against your
Shin—cells—chest—interlocked.
The jeans you wore—one night—and my tongue pressed a hole
through your cheek—and
now I taste blood—your liquid—fills my gut and I'm drunk
with desire—touch this passion—hand on neck—and I apply
tension so there is realization of the matter

I'm not your whore—always—but tonight I may allow an
exception—ill blow you apart and let you shower me clean
with your juices—neutralized beauty.

Tucker's notes demonstrate that not all suicide notes are, in
fact, the proverbial end. They are coping mechanisms to flesh out
complex, troubling, or bizarre feelings at a time in a teenager's
life when they are becoming, in many ways, their own person.
Throughout Tucker's story, and in his "suicide notes," he describes
being preoccupied with suicidal angst to such an extent that it
is frankly shocking that he is not dead. Yet Tucker transitioned
from his homicidal rages to becoming a postsuicidal young man
because he has resilience and wants to survive.

We do not know all the ways in which teens cope and survive.
We know some, but no true studies show definitively what accounts for any particular person's ability to withstand depression
and feelings of worthlessness and reemerge from the ashes of
despair.

Tucker's homosexual side was forcing him into depression,
and by the time adolescence hit, he was dealing with hormonal
issues as well. He was still being pressured by his father to have a
girlfriend, be a jock, and do well in school. The constant pressure
caused Tucker to resent the whole family, because he felt alone. It
was thus a long, festering depression that caused him to want to
end his life.

Clearly, Tucker was having issues with his homosexuality at a
very young age, and he could not talk to his parents about this at
all. I believe the resolution of this issue, via his film work, did allow him to see himself in whole terms for the first time.

Of the years during which he was preoccupied with suicide
and cutting, Tucker says:

That was a phase when I was trying to understand who I was, and having to deal with my sexuality, my manhood, my life at school and home as a teenage boy, all at the same time, and it was difficult. It was really a harrowing time for me, and I'm glad I'm over it. I'm glad I survived it, and I never want to be in that place again. I've made up with my parents, and they both love me, as I do them. We all grew up together, because they taught me some things and I taught them as well.

Today, Tucker is an amateur filmmaker whose first film looks promising as he explores older gay men and young boy love. His self-styled "underground manifesto to life as a young man" caused a stir at the college he attends, and he now works as a gay activist to improve the lives of gay men on his campus.

6

ESCAPING DEATH

Gita

Gita, sixteen years old, wrote in her diary:

Dear Mom,

I realize this year you were quite pissed with me, but I was more upset with you. I tried and tried, again and again to get us together, to try and make you see the real me. I tried to get you and dad to listen to me. Me! But it was you who refused. If you were trying to get back at me for the times I didn't wash my hair back to black from purple or I didn't throw away my Marilyn Manson music, or dump my friends so you could feel comfortable, fuck you. It's out of my control that I love Manson's music and think the world of my friends even if I go off the wall behind them. They are all I have.

I have tried to reach out to you but you never have enough time for me. You never want to listen to me. You never want to really get to know me. I want you to know that this letter is not meant to frighten you but to wake you up because the so-called "beautiful daughter" you had is now going to that Hell you always said I would end up in.

Gita

Those words began a harrowing journey for this teenager from Long Island, New York. Tall and skinny, with a small mole near her top lip, sharp features, and long, dark hair, Gita is a mix of two cultures, East Indian and Italian. She speaks with a Long Island accent and bends her words around the edges of her sentences.

In her note, Gita tells her parents they didn't listen to or love her enough, and she uses the note and journal writing to express deep seated feelings held inside for years. She explains:

> I didn't think killing myself was so bad. I thought I would show my parents that I was brave enough to do this horrible thing and punish them for what they did to me. Wait till you see what I wrote in my note. It was a blast, because they fucking deserve to see me stretched out, all pretty and dead, while they wail away, saying stupid shit like "I wish I had listened to her. I wish I had loved her more."

Gita intrigued me from the start because I was impressed by her quick intellect and striking sense of humor. At our first meeting, she spoke as if we had known each other for years, and she talked for several hours about her life and travails. She has bright, expressive eyes that immediately indicate her mood. They light up when she tells her story about the joys she's had, and just as quickly dim, the moment she recalls an account of her "bad times."

Verbally abused by parents and older siblings, Gita had been sexually molested, and she sought ways to deal with her hurt and shame. Attempted suicide was her most frequent method. I cannot verify some of the claims made by teenagers, such as when they report sexual molestation, but I am more apt to believe than to disbelieve them. Self-reports are always an issue when doing ethnographic work, but these kids usually believe and trust I will not harm them by revealing any information they want to keep private. The kids saw me as someone in whom they could confide.

Gita's suicide attempts ranged from drug overdoses to random sex with strangers, after risky rendezvous in midtown bars. Over the course of a year, Gita and I communicated in many ways—over the phone, in face-to-face interviews, through letters, and through passages from her journal, such as:

I am sixteen years old; my mom thinks I'm at a girlfriend's sleep-over party. By the looks of things, I'm afraid I'm not going to make it through the night because there is so much booze and drugs around. Life didn't really start for me until 1994. I am all decked out in my leather mini, combat boots, fishnet stockings, nose-ring, and black lipstick. I am ready to rock. I don't feel [like] myself when I'm not wearing black. I am at the Roxy in Huntington, Long Island—an old heavy metal club that's really just a dingy, crusty hole in the wall with a dilapidated garage door [for] its front entrance. This was to be one of the last concerts before the place was torn down.

I couldn't breathe. The tiny club is holding more than double its capacity. Some sweaty, obese guy at least three times my age is rubbing up against me in the mosh pit. I turn around in disgust and stamp on his foot. (I may have small feet, but [I have] big steel-toed shoes on.) Then I force my way to the front to get a glimpse of the opening act, the Lunachicks.

The lead singer, with knotty teased-out hair, a makeup disaster streaked all over her face, dressed in a red plastic dress, stuffs a microphone into her vagina on stage. The crowd boos and calls her a slut. It seems, perhaps because she's a woman, [that] they're just not ready for that yet.

But they are ready for someone else. The army of darkness begins to shout his name: "Manson! Manson!" They point their middle fingers, make devil horn signs with their hands, and shake their fists. Some of them chant, "We hate love! We love hate!" Beside me, a short, pale, emaciated girl with tattoos and short, spiky hair screeches out "Fuck you, Manson!" She then gazes at the stage, anticipating, with an evil smile.

Gita found solace in the lyrics of Marilyn Manson songs. She said:

His songs were so prophetic, because in one song he sings about rape, and that same year I heard the song I was raped by. It was the second time I had become a victim of sexual assault.

My mother and I were living in a lower-class rural neighborhood in Florida. At the time, my parents weren't divorced yet, but they might as well have been. She was out of work, we were on welfare, and her abusive alcoholic boyfriend's twelve-year-old daughter used to babysit me when our parents went out. I was six years old the first time I was abused, and it continued until I was seven.

Aside from her showing me pornography on television from their satellite dish, and once forcing me to watch our parents have sex from an outside window, she violated me over and over again in sexual ways. I told my mother I wanted to move back to live with my grandparents in the Long Island suburbs; I never told her exactly why.

Gita wrote in her journal:

Those in attendance are mostly in the same age group as her and me: below twenty-one. We're all drinking and smoking clove cigarettes. In my slightly buzzed state, the swaying, silky strings captivate me over a dozen wooden marionettes, eerily hung from both sides of the stage. The area is also littered with broken and beaten prosthetic arms and legs. Suddenly, the haunting sweet sounds of music boxes and carnival rides begin to play. The curtains open. My mouth, eyes, and mind open wide; I have never seen anything like this before.

Long-haired, skinny, covered in tattoos, scars, and pancake makeup, wearing eyeliner, lipstick, black nail-polish, and combat boots, naked except for the garter belt, stockings, and what appear to be ace bandages wrapped around his waist, Marilyn Manson emerges onto the stage.

He crouches and begins wriggling and thrusting convulsively to the beat he starts to sing: "I am the god of fuck . . ." His bassist, Twiggy Ramirez, is wearing a dress, giving us the look of death, and playing with a dangling arm that seems like it's about to break off from his body. The whole band is cross-dressed and covered in German Expressionist-like makeup; they look as if they just escaped from a mental hospital or a horror version of *Willy Wonka and the Chocolate Factory*.

I just can't get enough of it.

Before we learn to appreciate music for the individual drum riffs, creative consumption, and exceptional rhythms, we select our favorite songs based on how they make us feel. They mimic our innermost thoughts and feelings. We listen to ballads when we're sad, upbeat tempos when we want to feel good, and many forms of rap or heavy metal when we need to release pent-up rage, frustration, or deeply hidden love and desire. Gita speaks of Manson as her savior:

When I was about to give up on the world, Marilyn Manson and the Goth scene provided me with an escape from the realities of my inner teen hell. Depressing as the lyrics were, the music gave me hope, and the scene gave me the feeling that I was not alone. Rather, I began to feel part of something greater. To a teenager who had always felt like a reject, this was a fantastic feeling.

We Mansonites paid dearly for our devotions. I was thrown out of my house for days and forced to sleep in my friend's car for listening to *Portrait of an American Family*, Manson's first album.

My mother, grandmother, and stepmother were ashamed to walk out in public with me because of the Gothic style of fashion I adopted. I went to the clubs. My entire family assumed that I would amount to nothing, even though I was exceptionally creative, had top grades in my honors classes, and was involved in a slew of extracurricular activities, which, for me, were also an escape from my home life.

Goth, the scene Gita describes as a place where she feels truly herself, is a growing teen phenomenon in schools, in nightclubs, and on the Internet. The definitions of Goth offered by teenagers themselves are often very different from descriptions in the media, which pegs Goths as killers, bloodsuckers, or cult members. Eric Harris and Dylan Klebold, the teenagers who committed the brutal school shooting at Columbine High School, were called Goths in the media.

In the notes from Gita, we see in detail the Goth scene, its relations to social pressures and teenage identity, and its connections to death and violence. For these kids, it is nothing more than an escape and a comfort. Many of the kids I spoke with are interested in the world according to gangs, or the Goth or rave scenes, or hardcore music, or marijuana group hangouts, and they have made their interest known to parents and friend alike. At the same time, when they are asked whether they belong to such groups, all deny such associations.

Gita recalls, "At Thanksgiving, my mother and I had a three-day altercation about a music magazine with Marilyn Manson's picture on the cover that she saw me reading in my room." In addition to disapproval at home, Gita was mocked and jeered at in high school, as were other kids like her. One day, a public school student in nearby community, wearing clothes similar to Gita's style, was thrown down a flight of stairs and nearly killed for being a "freak." Soon after, some of the jocks and "gangsta" kids at Gita's high school formed a "master freak list" of one hundred people they were "out to get." It turned out she was number forty-nine on the list.

Gita notes:

Some of those on the list were not even real freaks but were listed simply because they associated with the freaks. [Because] of my treatment at home and threats I received in school, I was forced to tone done my outward appearance; however, I kept listening to the music.

I began sneaking out to shows and clubs in New York City to try to find my own "kind," and would keep extra clothes in my school locker so no one would find out. I told very few people about my little adventures.

But her adventures continued, as she reminds us in this excerpt from her journal:

At night I showed way too much cleavage, scraped at my wrists with razor-blades, head banged to Marilyn Manson, and hung out with and gave blow-jobs to long-haired heavy metal boys in bands. I had low self-esteem from kids ridiculing me and grabbing at my body, because my breasts developed early. I grew up to become a high school honor student, heavy-metal chick, filled with low self-esteem and contradictions.

I remained a virgin (no boy had ever penetrated me), and never did drugs really. Well, unless you consider alcohol a drug. I was scared that if I did those things, I would lose control and get myself killed.

Gita's problems at her high school, combined with issues at home, contributed to her state of being. She finally talked about the role her parents played in her young life at that time.

My parents were basically not functioning as parents, if you think about it. Listen, I had the absent father; I had the abusive boyfriend/lover of my mother; I had the freaky sex-maniac stepsister; I had the pre-divorce ritual trauma, and a few other oddities around me.

Until winter break of last year. I was visiting my dad (who I hardly see) and he had just gotten remarried to a religious fanatic who called me "the devil" to my face. I hopped on a bus and left his house in Massachusetts, hardly saying good-bye, just in time to enjoy New Year's Eve in New York City.

Once she arrived in the city, however, Gita found herself faced with a problem that had drastic consequences, which she recounted:

I had an alcohol problem at the time; the booze felt good going down when I wanted to forget about my problems with school, family, loneliness, hopelessness, uncertainty, my past, and feelings of worthlessness. I met a guy hanging out with his father at a college bar, the West End. They bought me some drinks. I found out the dad was a prominent member of the administration at a local college; he was even best friends with the dean of a prestigious law school I was thinking of applying to one day.

I lied about my identity and told them I was a law student (after all, there I was, drinking under age, right in front of the administration).

The father left and the guy told me about his dad's current affair. That Daddy had a history of cheating on Mommy. The guy almost started to cry. I quickly changed the subject. He bought me some more drinks. I tried to stand up and fell off the bar stool. He offered to walk me home. I confessed who I really was, and that I was only seventeen.

He confessed that he was nineteen. He claimed he had a really cool dad who let him have a drink with him once in a while. I believed him; he did look like he could pass for nineteen. I admit I was attracted to the guy. I even gave him my number, but I had no intention of allowing him to do what he did to me after he walked me home.

He offered to "help" me into my dorm room. I trusted him. After all, I could barely creep up the stairs. The dorms were deserted; everyone had gone home for the holidays. After we got inside, he raped me.

After hearing this, I asked her to explain what happened after that.

I did not have the courage or clearheadedness to report what happened. I convinced myself that if I told anyone, no one would believe me. Like so many other victims of rape, I began to blame myself. Rape is the one crime in which everything is taken from you. Everything about you has been violated. You are left practically without any kind of rationale or control.

The weeks following the rape— in a manner of speaking—I went crazy. I got piercings in both my nipples, as well as my genitals, all at the same time. I brought a different stranger up to my room every night. Not for sex, but just to mess around and to not feel alone. I wasn't thinking about what might happen to me, about my future. At that point, I didn't care if one of those guys decided to kill me and cut me up into little pieces.

I wanted to end my life, but did not have the guts to do it myself. I just wanted to feel in control again, to act as if nothing had happened. I wanted to forget about everything and get rid of the confusion and numbness I was experiencing, and so I wrote my first suicide note.

Gita went on a spending binge to assuage her anxiety about the rape.

The last straw for me was when I got some credit card bills in the mail [totaling more than] five thousand dollars. Now not only was I in search of sexual power and self-worth, I also desperately needed to get money, fast (to pay back the card debt). I could have gotten a job at McDonald's or taken out a loan. But I would not have been able to punish myself for the rape, nor be able to punish my parents for ignoring and harassing me, nor regain a sense of sexual control with any of those options. So, instead, I tried to be a dominatrix.

It is interesting how Gita's dysfunctional family life led to her other problems: being raped, having all sorts of illicit sex, becoming a dominatrix, and basically being totally out of control, trying to deal with her pain.

When that didn't work out as a dominatrix, I became a stripper. It was a conscious choice; no one forced me into it. Past boyfriends and other men had encouraged me to become a stripper. They said things like, "Hell, if I were a girl and I had a body like yours, I'd do it." At the time, I thought of it as a compliment. I, like them, had an illusion of astronomical cash.

All my friends were gone on vacation and I had no one to talk to. I had never been close enough to my parents, who would have been destroyed by the stories I had to tell. I knew I could not ask them for money, either; they were barely making it as it was. It was up to me to find a way out of this mess.

Gita decided to start stripping and to do what many young girls were doing to make "easy money." One night, after hearing about a club hiring teenagers—with or without identification— she made it to a small, dingy, dank-smelling dive. "I could smell the basement before I could see it. It was the stench of filth, human ejaculation [from the activities of prostitutes and their tricks], rotting walls and floorboards, pot and crack smoking, and stagnant water from an overflowed toilet."

Gita performed her first show after being given the tour of the place and directed down a narrow, dilapidated stairway by a buxom, British bisexual named "Nibbles" (whom she later befriended). The scene downstairs was a sharp contrast to the elegant grooming rituals of the strippers she'd watched in the upstairs VIP club room. Instead, she says:

> This reminded me of a description of a restaurant and the kitchen: back of the house. It is a marked departure from the main dining area, I was placed among a group of strippers sitting on broken chairs and smoking crack. One girl was crying as she did the drug, tears rolling down her face in big drops. Another girl in a bathroom stall was sobbing and yelling loudly. She was having problems urinating. "I can't even fuckin' pee!" she screamed, because she got "something from some asshole."
>
> Another stripper was brushing her teeth in the sink, above a broken mirror. She had evidently just left the back room, where a man could essentially get anything he wanted for three hundred dollars, even a complimentary bottle of champagne.
>
> By the end of that night, I had gotten drunk, gotten on stage, and finally, got a job. But I was not happy about what I had "achieved," because I was guilty, confused, angry, depressed, sad, empty, sweaty, scared, and tired. Most of all, I felt dirty and completely degraded. But I thought that was what a slut like me deserved.
>
> I used all the money I made from my one dance on stage toward a cab ride to my dorm. I could not even pay for the whole thing. The driver let me out at Seventy-Second Street. I took the subway the rest of the way home and cried myself to sleep.
>
> The clients always used to tell me that a girl like me didn't belong in that place. But I don't think anyone belongs in a place like that. I wanted to die.

Gita didn't think killing herself was such a bad option at the time. She thought it would show her parents that she was brave enough to do this horrible thing and to punish them for what they did to her. She wrote six more suicide notes but never did anything—though not, as she saw it, because she didn't have reason.

> I'm glad I didn't kill myself. I know it sounds weird, but I'm kinda happy, because I think that was just a phase in my life. It was just a time when I was at the lowest point, because I couldn't see a way out.

We can see the difficulty in kids' attempts to fix their own problems. Yet those attempts are the first signs of coming out of the suicidal cycle, and most kids need help from caring adults, counselors, clinicians, and others capable of seeing and understanding the trauma they are facing. As Gita and other kids write in diaries and journals and/or talk about their situations with friends, they are actually in the process of curing themselves, because they are employing a mechanism by which they can change their behavior.

Teens like Gita, who complain of feeling worthless and alone, may begin drinking or using drugs heavily, and this increases the risk of suicide. Among at-risk school-age youth, girls are more likely than boys to have suicidal thoughts, to create a suicide plan, and to attempt suicide, though boys more often succeed in committing the act. This relation between gender, suicide, and suicide attempts is significant.

Where we work, how we dress, who we befriend, and how we speak and act are points of pride for most teenagers, because these things allow them to safely express their innermost thoughts and feelings. We are all walking billboards, advertising who we are on the inside, so most teenagers going through difficult times see themselves as already showing parents, teachers, and friends the problems and issues they deal with on a daily basis. All they ask in return is that someone actually stands up and takes notice.

Gita is smart, but also lucky. She is fortunate not to have been killed during this period in her life, because even though she sought out these harrowing experiences—and may even have wanted to die at the time—it was a temporary emotion.

Like Tucker (chapter 5), Gita ended up more or less able to cope. Her story is a tour de force of dark emotions and transactions, and then suddenly the dark tunnel of emotions opens up and we are in the light. I wonder, however, if there is some kind of epiphany, when dealing with suicidal ideations, that enables a teenager to forego committing suicide. This is an important part of the narrative, and these ideas are included in the journals to the degree that they are aligned with the interpretive interlocutor voice of the ethnographer. This strikes me as important in the context of Gita's narrative, which, like Tucker's story, seemingly ends quickly. But these young people came into my life with such urgency and, in a way, without warning, and they left just as abruptly.

I have provided more information about Gita's background than about the background of some other kids because I found out more about her East Indian and Italian life than I found out about others. East Indian and Italian heritage is really specific, as opposed to, say, East Indian and white. I did not probe into the background of all the kids because I was there to listen, and I listened a lot. I was building trust, and part of the structure was to probe gently, as a person sincerely trying to hear them rather than as a sociologist probing for information. If they told me about themselves, I recorded it, but if they chose not to, I left it alone.

Trust is very important in this work, and the worst thing a researcher can do is to fail to be trusted. Through all the work I've done in this adolescent ethnography, building trust is paramount, and the kids know this by my reputation. Once I established that trust, Megan (chapter 3) and others trusted me to tell their stories. I only regret that it took so long to get their stories out. When I noticed certain information was missing from my field notes, I would try to get that information the next time I got the chance, but usually I ended up not pressing those issues. In most cases, I never got a third or fourth chance to inquire, because the kids were gone.

At the time of my research, I didn't feel the need to know the demographics. I was not doing a sociological study so much as a series of stories about kids who were willing to take me into their confidence and tell me everything about themselves. I ended up with a good deal of information about Gita's ethnic background, her age, where she grew up—key pieces of demography—though this information is uneven in the other narratives.

Moreover, I found Gita's narrative to be very poignant—almost surreal—but quite informative. Her journal provides very specific information about Goth culture, Marilyn Manson, and music, all of which can be tied to a specific time frame and culture. Yet there is so much missing information, and assumptions made about middle-class family life, that this narrative blows the roof off the notion that pathology, as such, is the sole province of the ghetto—that is, black folks and other collective personae non gratae. Furthermore, what does it mean to have two parents (as the ideal model of American family life), if adolescent alienation is in some cases unavoidable? Because the stories in this narrative transpired in the 1990s, I think it is crucial to place them within a cultural frame of reference (music, parental ideas, and religious upbringing) to give it greater utility in the literature about teen-age suicide.

I gave a great deal of thought to these narratives, from a methodological perspective. Clearly, as Gita indicates, the revelations in her journal (her "suicide notes") would have been too much for her parents to bear.

Gita admits:

I made some mistakes, and I've learned from them. And I know I made some narrow escapes, too. But the thing is, if I hadn't made those mistakes I would have never been the person I am now.

I am nobody. Nobody is me.
And yet - I can't keep being me. Can I ?. It's
unbearable how long it takes me to find a way out.
I want to laugh at myself for being so ridiculous,
trying over and over again, trying to find a way out,
trying to accept my situation, trying to make the best
out of it, as [illegible] society's terror seems to echo.
Hoping for [future] to kiss me awake like the prince
in the Sleeping Beauty. I don't just want to sleep,
though.
Picturing myself dying, in a way I chose myself
seems so comforting, healing and brave. I'd look
at my wrists and watch the blood seeping, I'd
be a spectator in my last act of self - determination.
By having lost all my self respect it seems like
the last pride I own, determining the time I die.
I [struggle] too long to buy their shit. Medication?
To live in a brave new world?
Dying doesn't hurt. Living does. I don't feel like
I'm alive anyway. I couldn't tell the difference,
except for I'd be released of my pain.
I reached the point where I don't care about other
people anymore I used to be across so sensitive to
realize when a breeze [turned] into a storm. Now
it's their turn to feel guilty and helpless.
Now it's their [turn] of tasting [illegible]
failure, of self hate that corrodes your soul until
the ultimate self-destruction.

A DIARY ENTRY BY KYRA.

Terri Williams
Graduate Faculty
of Political and Social Science
65 Fifth Avenue
New York, NY. 10003

Terri,

Thank you for allowing me to be in this book. Though I did not open-up to the city I still in some way enjoyed my short stay.

Sorry I've waited so long to mail this to you. See I am the great procrastinator and it is my nature to wait. However, I do have a question and I don't want to sound rude. But, I was wondering if the seventy-five you gave me was my payment-in-full. Not that I feel anything is owed to me, I'm just in a bind and my mind happened to drift back

there. Also, do you still have contact w/ ___? Because, if so I would like for you to give him my adress & phone # the next time you-two speak. Thank you Terri.

P.S. also contact me when the book comes out.

A LETTER FROM ENOCH.

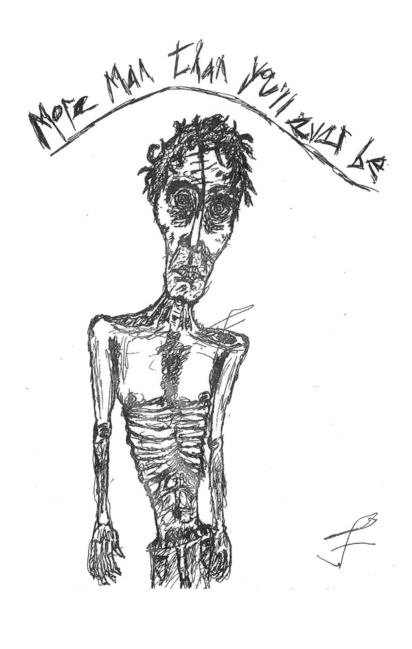

A DRAWING BY ENOCH.

Dear Mom,

I'm sorry I ended up such a big disapointment.

love,

DAVID'S SUICIDE NOTE.

2/27/96

i can no longer contain myself inside these walls –
you fucking faggot, you fucking faggot, you
fucking faggot, you fucking faggot, you faggot –
and my sight becomes blurred as i
stare into his eyes – beautiful sin – i
touch my lips – so gently to your cheek – and
employ my tongue – pressing against
your skin – cells & chests – interlocked
like jeans you wore – one night – and
my tongue pressed a hole through your
cheek – and now i taste blood –
your liquid – fills my guts and i am
drunk with desire – touch this
passion – hand on neck – and i apply
tension so there is realization of the matter –
i am not your whore – always – but to night
i may make an exception – i'll blow you
apart – and let you shower are – clean –
with your juices & nutralized beauty...

6/22/01   PAGE 1

after a long stay in hotel minesota. i am getting ready to leave.
erica & i are in minot, north dakota, waiting in some hidden corner
of the park which we have made our temporary camp. we are
going to catch a freight train tonight headed to seattle, which will take
anywhere from two - six days, we stocked up on food & beer with
money that was given to us in minnesota. actually, its kind of
funny & disturbing how we got the money. . . .
we were sitting on an on ramp trying to catch a ride and a
girl & a guy pull up about 50 feet away. she says that she is not
going our way being local, but she could give us $10 dollars. so
erica gave her a hug. "jesus loves you" was the girls words as
she got back to the passenger seat & drove away. so we kept
hitchin' about 10 minutes older, she came back with more money
in her hand. "we were a little stingey before, because we only
gave you $10 but jesus loves you more than that so here is
$30 more". then erica came back & told me that we hugged for
quite awhile . . .
"jesus loves you more than that"

_____

we had spent about a month in minnesota except for us gracing
fargo with our presence for a week.
we went: mineapolis, mn (8 days) to deluth, mn (3 days) to
mineapolis (3 days) to fargo, nd (6 days) to min. (8 days)
this month was one of unprecedented debauchery for the traveling
community. every day we drank hundreds of dollars worth of beer
(using funds we begged from complete strangers) one of the nights
we stayed at some kids apartment (16 of us & 3 dogs) everybody
drank naked all night . . . there was no wild orgies, as the reefer
madness propaganda of the fifties would imply, but there was an
odor so strong that it could make birds fall dead from the sky.
there was fielding, mad diving, puking, spitting, lice, people getting drunk
on with marker for passing out with their shoes on (which is a
well known custom among new gypsies like ourselves) loud music and
of course your average small dick contest. the festival in fargo that
we went to was said to be the "olympics of drinking" by time magazine →

_____

A LETTER FROM CODY.

im not sorry that i did this. i don't have any
reason to be...
        i can no longer endure the pain. life is abuse.
i have felt suffocated for so long. i have been taught
to be ashamed for thinking, for feeling. it is not
even possible for me to control my own life anymore.
my control has been auctioned off to ~~another thing~~
some omnipotent force that im afraid we have
created. i can't stand facing what we are & what
we have made. yes, cancer & garbage disposals
will get you, yes the world is a terrible place,
yes a war is coming, the world's shot to hell
& you're all goners. your fear, your own lives are
your entertainment. i just need to turn it off.
one can only hold on for so long before letting
go.
        we have strayed so far and i can't find
my way back.

p.s. hopefully work will allow you to take
a day off for my burial.

A JOURNAL ENTRY BY GABRIELLA.

6/7/96

BROWNSON'S CODED LETTER.

7

SHOCK JOCK

Boots

Boots, a Long Island boy, wrote:

If my parents ever found out about me cross-dressing I would kill myself. I would fucking die right then and there. One day they almost did, and I was preparing myself. At the time I would have preferred it not to have been a part of myself. Being hung up and not coming to terms with something is counterproductive. So for the sake of self-realization I realized the existence of my love for silk, velvet, and odd-colored make-up. That's why I wrote that note.

I met Boots in New York City one cold winter day as he sat waiting to enter a classroom. I was recruiting kids for my Writers Crew Project at The New School by offering an experimental course called The Organic Novel, in which I asked ten kids to cowrite a novel based on personal experiences. Boots, a recent high school graduate with long, curly hair, sandals, and jeans, sat yoga style, legs crossed and confident, in a corner of the room. He wears horn-rimmed glasses and a sharp grin crosses his face when something amusing or off-putting is said. He told me his interests are "writing, poetry, and life. I've been told they're all the same. I thought maybe you could help me find out if there's any difference."

Boots, ten days shy of his eighteenth birthday, hangs out mostly in the East Village, where he reads poetry in an underground workshop, smokes pot, and attends dances with a mixed bag of friends, from tween skateboarders to aging hippie writers, in a world oblivious to his parents. He tried several times to commit suicide, because of problems with his parents, teachers, school, and himself. In high school he was a social recluse, and the extracurricular activities he chose to engage in consumed all his time and energy.

Although Boots is a healthy heterosexual male, his interest in cross-dressing places him at risk of being labeled a "faggot." Indeed, his proclivity may be only a stage in his life, but friends and peers, if they are kind, will most likely see him as different.

Most of the people I knew, with a few exceptions, marginally interested me. I felt people were trite and boring. So I spent most of my time in school reading in the back of class, in empty classrooms during lunchtime, and on the sidelines with the en vogue girls who flirted with the jocks in gym class.

Of all the kids I saw that day, Boots was by far the most interesting and eager to share his journals, poetry, and writing with me. After several meetings, during which we talked about his life and family, he described one of the first incidents of attempting to harm himself. He began with odd uses of household drug combinations. He says to me, rather matter-of-factly and with an impish grin:

I knew I could die if the experiment didn't go right. My parents were away. I believe it was Memorial Day weekend. I mixed the drugs with nutmeg, some ice cream, in a blender, because it seems to be the easiest form of ingestion—you don't taste it that much. I didn't feel anything the first time, and so I decided to double the dose. I wanted to shut down my nervous system, numb my brain, and the last thing I remember was lying down on the bed before passing out. My body had shut down.

I never really thought any more specifically about how I would kill myself than that. Except one time I thought about dressing up and jumping off a building in Times Square on New Year's Eve.

I tried to OD again one time, because I believed that dying was not what I had been taught. I had a ritual all figured out. I mean, I was just preparing in my head about how I wanted to die. I took the same portion, but put exactly four tablespoons of nutmeg—this is 1.8 ounces—two tablets of Benadyrl, and mixed it up into a banana milkshake.

I was into Gnosticism and the focus on the devotion to certain exercises, usually under the guide of a teacher. Now, these ritual exercises can be fasting, meditation, or ritual drug taking. I chose drug taking without a teacher. I believe the human body dies only because we have forgotten how to transform it and change it.

Boots is an enigma. Although he is heterosexual, his proclivity for dressing in women's clothes created a deep dark secret he did not wish anyone, especially his parents, to find out about. He also recalled, almost apologetically, a situation that created waves in the family when he was a kid:

I remember when the "bedding incident" happened, and my father was away at the time. And I was so nervous and scared and anxious, for days it seemed, waiting to hear my fate. I might as well tell you what happened there, because it got out of our house and followed me to therapy, because my sister told the therapist one day by accident.

Anyway, the thing was, one night when my dad was away, my sister and me started playing doctor and nurse and I ended up falling asleep in her bed with the doctor's stethoscope. Hell, I was only eight then, and she was ten, but my mom said the "instrument," as she called it, was between my sister's legs, and she (my mother) was horrified.

She screamed and pulled me outta the bed and called my grandmother in Florida and tried to reach my father, who was in Europe, I think, at the time. So when my dad got back he asked me what happened, and I told him we were playing but nothing happened like mom had said—and by now the "incident" had turned to some kind of incest, rape, horror story. Anyway, my mom said something had to be done, so they sent me, then my sister, to therapy. My dad just ignored me more than anything else, and that really annoyed me and made me feel like shit.

My dad was nothing if not efficient—efficiently late, efficiently proper, efficiently absent. This is not to say he wasn't a good provider. Please don't let my cynicism make him out to be a totally bad person, because he wasn't. He was like a lot of fathers in the 'burbs, in America really. He did his duty and showed everyone around that he was the man of the house, brought home the bacon, drove the Mercedes station wagon, sat in on Thanksgiving dinner and Christmas present time and all of that. But was he the perfect dad? No. There are no perfect dads.

My father worked for a [French] company—selling bonds, I later found out. And he was gone a lot during my childhood. I was left alone by him for most of my teen years. Then, when my mom would dote over me, he would say I was being spoiled, that she was spoiling me. My mom accused my father of being the cause of problems in our family because he was never at home to help take care of his kids and all of that. Most of their arguments was around her spending too much of her time with her friends, and he was just being absent altogether. My mother was a housewife, who dressed up and had her friends over and they talked and gossiped all the time. The biggest arguments they had was around his going away so much and not taking her or us with him except at vacation time. She would say there is no such thing as giving a kid too much affection. But my dad was basically awkward around his kids, and he never really was very affectionate with my mother, either. Of course, he would buy me stuff, lots of toys and things.

Parents usually live to regret the decisions they make about their kids. Especially if the kid commits suicide or behaves badly later in life. And parents *should* feel bad, because it was those priorities, those decisions they made to exclude their kids, because they thought the kids should be on their own or felt the kids' issues could wait until a later time, and then time ran out.

I believe Boots really means *his* parents will regret the decisions they make regarding *him* if *he* decides to commit suicide. He's anticipating coming out as a transvestite but has reservations. He believes his parents should feel bad if they reject him when he does come out and finally leave home. He blames his parents for his dilemma, because they made the decision to send him to the church school and it was in the church school that the "dressing up" started.

When Boots began to explain this situation, his voice took on a slightly animated tone. Suddenly his boyish, raffish, tough look becomes a more girly demeanor, the long hair falling in his face, the big eyes wide open and expressive. He begins, almost in a whisper, telling me about being traumatized by a priest.

The priest told me if I continued to act up he would put me in the "dark room," which I learned was a walk-in closet in the basement of the school. He did put me there, but he did more than that. One day he told me to put on these little-girl dresses, because I had been so bad. I sat there for an hour or more, this first time and every time after that. If I'd act up, he'd do this same thing to me. He told me not to say anything to my parents or I'd be sent to hell.

Ironically, as articulate as Boots is, this was the first time he seemed at a loss for words. He sat there in front of me, frozen, with a blank stare, looking at the wall and trying to find the right words. I wondered why he never mentioned this before and whether this was the source of his dressing up, but he didn't say it was. Nor did he say the priest did anything sexual during these encounters. But the humiliation of being locked in the closet and made to wear little-girl clothes has had a lasting effect, and his cross-dressing became one of the ways his sexuality developed.

He began to be confused about his sexuality. He saw the priest as honest in his affection for him, because the priest complimented him on how he looked in girls' clothing, but the priest also spanked Boots if he acted out. These contradictory situations created even more confusion in the young boy. He heard other boys whispering about the "dark room," and they would snicker and giggle at him when he came back from the encounters. When the spankings stopped, Boots felt a betrayal of the pact he thought he and the priest had, and self-doubt and hurt, mixed with shame, overwhelmed him. "Maybe after a while I'd act up just to be there in that room, but I don't really know. I also don't know why I never told my parents or my teacher."

Boots was both humiliated and uncertain about what to do, because he was a kid caught in a strange situation. If he told his teacher, he would be further humiliated, or called a liar, because the teachers and priests were one and the same, and if he told his parents, he felt he'd be yelled at and blamed. He felt alone and abandoned.

According to Walter Torres and Raymond Bergner, "Suffering severe humiliation has been shown empirically to plunge individuals into major depressions, suicidal states, and severe anxiety states, including ones characteristic of post-traumatic stress disorder."[1] When the humiliation, shame, and anger get to be too much; when no one seems to be listening to what kids go through, hearing their words, or watching their habits; when they feel trapped, alone, left behind, and begin to question the very society they've prayed would notice and help them, it can create a catastrophic situation. In the worst instances, when smart and creative children yearn to grow but simply cannot, and when they begin to blame those around them instead of taking responsibility for what they can, some kids hurt not only themselves but also others around them, expressing a rage and torment completely incomprehensible to the outside world. One such incident was the Columbine shooting, which Boots references:

> I think parents stop prioritizing their kids because they want to get back to their life, they feel they're given enough and now it's their time to live out the last remaining years, free of the burdens of children. But what the parents of many of these suicide victims forget is that their kids always needed them. Sometimes I feel like the kid from Columbine.

The suicide note left by Columbine shooter Eric Harris reads:

> By now, it's over. If you are reading this, my mission is complete . . .
> Your children who have ridiculed me, who have chosen not to
> accept me, who have treated me like I am not worth their time are

dead. THEY ARE FUCKING DEAD . . . Surely you will try to blame
it on the clothes I wear, the music I listen to, or the way I choose to
present myself, but no. Do not hide behind my choices. You need
to face the fact that this comes as a result of YOUR CHOICES.
Parents and teachers, you fucked up. You have taught these kids
to not accept what is different. YOU ARE IN THE WRONG. I have
taken their lives and my own—but it was your doing. Teachers,
parents, LET THIS MASSACRE BE ON YOUR SHOULDERS UNTIL
THE DAY YOU DIE.

I find this formulation interesting, even if it is considered a
fake suicide note. Are teachers, in the aftermath of this and more
recent shootings—such as that which occurred at Sandy Hook
Elementary, for example—trained to look for signs that would
lead an adolescent to walk into a school and commit mass murder
in the name of not being accepted in school or at home? I also
wonder whether there is a subtext of bullying here, because there
is a hierarchy of who is cool and popular among teenagers.

Boots says:

Until the time I was ten, every night before going to bed, I would
read horror stories and accounts of hauntings, alien abductions,
and the like. It was something I related to very closely with. I frequently had intense and vivid dreams. Often, in symbolic form,
things were revealed to me that would have a great influence on
the rest of my life. And I learned how to manipulate these things
for my advantage. Or there were the dreams where I floated
through strange landscapes—forests, hillsides, valleys, down dark
cobblestone city streets lined with decrepit vacant buildings.

The constant repetition of the Christian ethic in school, and
the feelings associated with being bad by dressing in girls' clothes,

turned Boots into a devout Lutheran with a compulsive hand-washing problem. Teachers would imply he was not supposed to think or behave in certain ways, but he couldn't keep himself from thinking about what he was not supposed to be thinking about or what he was not supposed to do. So, "I'd think of ways of maiming or killing people, what uses I could put fire to, what nasty little things I might say to people to hurt them—all that good stuff. Every time I'd have such a thought, I was compelled to wash my hands—be like Pontius Pilate."

The Bible, or religion in general, has been the source of many self-injurers' problems. Particularly relevant are the texts of Mark 9:43–48 and Matthew 5:29–30, which instruct Christian followers to tear out an eye or cut off an offending hand, since losing part of one's body is better than being cast whole into hell.[2]

Boots clearly had God-related issues, but he also had unresolved concerns about homosexuality and heterosexuality. He spoke about these things, reflecting on a childhood reference to religious ideas and its relationship to the body:

> I was a wiseass in [my church], and everybody treated me like I was a weakling or something. Like some gay nonfighter. So for a month and a half I got beat up. But for the most part the kids didn't fight. They were afraid of getting in trouble with their parents, so they just talked a lot of trash and dissed each other. I wasn't especially good at being the macho boy but I could hold my ground. But verbally, I'd cut those dim-witted kids down in a minute.
>
> On one occasion, I had some kid by the shirt and stopped myself midpunch, deciding it wasn't at all worth it. Besides, there was a lot of, "If you fuck with me you fuck with TCS," or whatever crew they belonged to. I had no one to back me up.

Boots decided early in school that the best approach to take with the bullies and the priests was to fight back with whatever tool was available. For the bullies, it was a verbal display and smart-aleck remarks, especially with words he knew they had no way of understanding. For the priests, it was the ultimate blasphemy: satanism. In his graffiti-covered journal Boots wrote: "In search for a cosmology that would affirm and explain my conjectures, I turned to Satanism."

He explains:

Satanism was what I was most warned about in [my church]. So I figured that the Lutherans were trying to keep me from exactly that which could liberate me and give free range to my imagination. I could not have been more correct in this assumption.

In another passage, he wrote, in red ink:

The so-called "Black Arts" is exactly what broke down the barrier between my reality and the one I was faced with waking up to every day. Through *The Satanic Bible*, the fiction of H. P. Lovecraft, and another book I have too much respect for to list the title, I learned that the particular brand of thought pattern I occasionally had whereby I tried to change the outside world, elicit certain states of mind, or manifest as corporeal what was at first conception not, was utilized by those who wrote these books.

These were people who had similar experiences to my own and dedicated themselves to interpreting what they "saw," then through their writings made the connections to what these things signified in consensus reality, which, by no small stretch of their imagination, they could corroborate through practical formulae and/or techniques.

Boots didn't speak of suicide as much after this spiritual encounter, and the reason he did not commit suicide was because
he was accepted by friends far away from his suburban home, and
because of his religious conversion. In Greenwich Village, where
alternative lifestyles are the norm, Boots felt relieved of the "small
town" pressure. He no longer had to keep secret his desires and
thus bear the burden of having to hold all those emotions inside.
This is interesting, and it raises the question of small suburban
towns and expected conformity versus the alternate, cosmopolitan world of Greenwich Village, a gay ghetto where he could fit
in. It is not, however, simply big city versus small town, because
there clearly are places in New York City where Boots would not
have fit in, either, and where the machinery of conformity is just
as acute.

Although the Village is not very far from Boots's suburban
home in terms of distance, it's light years away in attitude, values,
and acceptance of alternative lifestyles. You could argue it is an
alternate space, this ghetto of another kind—or, more properly
put, a "subghetto"—where alternate lifestyles can prosper. There
is a thriving gay community, and artists from all over the world
have settled there. In many ways, Boots needed time to define
and reflect on his own values, and the time spent in the Village
made him feel less alone and more part of a special community.
He experienced no environmental resistance, because many clubs
catered to his needs as well.

Instead of being a hostile environment, this change to a
friendlier place, where poets, writers, and queer others lived, en-
abled Boots to embrace a diverse culture, made him less stressed,
and relieved him of thinking about killing himself. This is important for another reason, too. New York City—and this may be
true of all large American cities—is a place of the great American

individual makeover, a place where one can reinvent oneself. This theme of reinvention is common in a city like New York, and one can even see this idea in American films. In the film *American Hustle*, for example, one of the female characters says that she came to New York to be anything other than what she was. In the suburbs and at home, Boots didn't see himself as bad, but he knew others did. He now found time to believe in his spirituality, and with that new belief, and the change of place, was helped to believe in himself.

Boots explains that this is why he didn't kill himself:

> For one thing I, was sustained by friends and my new family. I was going through a phase. I found religion. I found my passion (poetry). I found a support group of other poets, writers, queers. I admit this was just a phase many kids go through. It was basically my own special rite of passage.

Boots does what he refers to as his "poetry act" in a small Greenwich Village coffeehouse, where he reads and does automatic writing with a group of writers, poets, and other literary habitués. He admits to never being fazed by his teenage problems with suicide:

> I was in a state of grace, really. I was never really in any trouble with all of that. I knew who I was then, like I know who I am now. Nobody can live in this culture and not be a little confused, at least some of the time in their life, and I went through my dark period.

Boots admits that, today, his cross-dressing is reserved for parties and special occasions. He is completing a novel about his life in what he calls the "netherworld of nylon, silk, and panty hose."

In a journal Boots shared, he wrote:

To those closest to me. To those who don't dare to understand me. I have been cross-dressing since I was thirteen. I did it because I wanted to be as beautiful as the woman I saw in my fantasies. And I'd really turn myself on, too. I'd sit on my bed in pantyhose and a skirt I took from my sister's room, doing my math homework and listening to the Kinks—thinking I was just Divine.

After I got out of those clothes, I had a very hard time admitting to myself that I enjoyed it. I did not at all allow myself to acknowledge that I dressed in drag and occasionally preferred to act feminine. It didn't help much that I watched Charles Bronson and Clint Eastwood movies every night. I tried to model my thoughts and even my posture after that tough-guy hard-ass image.

I'd puff my chest out, walk with a swagger, try to make my voice deeper—even though at the time I probably wanted nothing more than to walk down the hall in school in a red dress, strappy shoes, and make-up, giving everyone nasty looks.

It wasn't so much that I agreed with and liked this side of myself.

I remember one day in April '99, looking back into my life, when I looked into the full-length mirror my parents had in their bedroom next to the window when I was maybe three or four years old. I was peeling a scab off my forehead. A few days earlier I had tripped on the sidewalk and fallen on my face running up the block to greet my grandparents, who had come to visit.

I picked at the scab because it stung every time I peeled a little more of it off. It didn't make any sense to me that I should feel pain. The pain was foreign and an intrusion on the flux of thoughts I was accustomed to thinking.

At that early age I was able to distinguish that, apart from apprehending the world; my stream of consciousness had no relation to it. What felt like the pain had no connection, no consanguinity with the world, as I knew it. I realized that the outside world was responsible for the pain I felt, and what I saw reflected before me in the mirror, was separate from myself and only subliminally responsible for what I was conscious of.

After all, most of what I was conscious of at that age was not particularly related to what my five senses picked up. From what I remember, I was most conscious of the abstract colors of my imagination, which were excited and intensified whenever I listened to one of my father's records. It then occurred to me what I was: a collection of spare parts—eyes, ears, nose, arms, legs, topped by a mop of black hair.

It wasn't much of a contrast from what I was seeing every day on *Sesame Street* and *Mr. Rogers' Neighborhood*. The only difference was that I didn't have blue skin or magenta fur. Even though I saw what everyone called "Little Bootsy" in the mirror, I did not feel that what I sensed myself to be was that reflection. I felt alien to this world then and I feel alien now.

I think one of the key points in Boots's narrative is the idea of individual reinvention. I was not prepared for this when I started reading from the kids' diaries, journals, and letters as a whole, but there is, in a sense, more redemption than anything else. One has to traverse through the narrative to understand parasuicidal ideation as a phase in the lives of some teenagers. This point is made throughout, but the title of the present book, coupled with what most people think of as a suicide note, does not really prepare one to see suicidal ideations as a prelude to redemption or coming to terms with deep emotional or familial issues.

Gay teens make up about 35 percent of all suicides committed each year, according to a report by the American Association of Suicidology. In 2011, 4,822 youths (age fifteen to twenty-four) died by suicide, making this the second leading cause of death among that age group. The same study reports that 38 percent of lesbian women and 35 percent of gay men (out of five thousand homosexuals) have attempted suicide. Psychotherapist Susan Kornblum told me that "the isolation gay teenagers experience is often hidden behind feelings of worthlessness and shame."

I did not want to ask Boots about the suicide notes again, so I was relieved when he brought the subject up.

> You wanted to know about the suicide notes I wrote? But I wonder if you heard about this twelve-year-old boy that I found on the Net. The kid left a suicide note telling his parents to watch the cartoon show *South Park* to learn why he killed himself.

I told him I had heard this, and I asked whether he was influenced at all by the twelve-year-old's suicide.

> No, I'm not influenced by it. But I'll be willing to bet that the parents and the police will blame the show for the death of the boy, and not the parents. They will blame everybody and everything but themselves.

As we move into the next century, young people like Boots, Gita, Enoch, Jill (who we will meet in chapter 8), and all the others will demand more recognition as a social category. They will present themselves as a self-identified collective, aware of their many differences but bound together by one important element: age. But identity, as these young people see it, has several levels. The main issue of identity is how Boots and Gita, for instance, perceive themselves, and then how others perceive them. For those young people, identity is a problem. As author and social activist bell hooks suggests, "Identity is complicated because it's based on sexuality, gender, class, race, territory, occupation, or whatever matters in one's individual and/or collective history."[3]

For these youths, and for most of the white kids in the book, "whiteness" is problematic. This is particularly true among white male teenagers, whose desire to be masculine is unresolved and often is played out through violence. While Boots contends with masculine issues of how to be a "man," Gita, for example, struggles with the problem of how to cope with being a "violated woman"—a stigma that is more internal than external. Nonetheless, they both confront the universal questions of identity: Who am I and where do I fit?

Boots tells me he had no interest in "controlling outcomes and circumstances," as he put it, and only concerned himself with a search "for truth, and not a quest for power." He found a world in books—which is to say he wanted to break down all barriers by doing what his so-called social conditioning forbade. His cross-dressing may be his true gender identity and his sincerest expression of individuality. He found himself using his imagination to help him work through the issues that bothered him the most, such as silly prejudices and stereotypes of gays, lesbians, and transgender people.

> When I wasn't sleeping, I was reading. One of the things my studies did for me was to make me hypersensitive. Certain sounds, smells, and shades of light make me want to violently lash out or have some sort of facial tick. It took great deal of self-control to keep myself outwardly composed and calm while my mind made

the most displeasing, repulsive connections. It would take me sometimes a few minutes to counterbalance and still my mind. So I would take four or five Benadryl to tranquilize me. I'd go into class, sit down, and in the next moment I would be waking up out of the void of my consciousness, slipped into just as the bell rang and class was over.

8

CUTTER

Jill

Jill, eighteen years old, wrote this note:

> I fall through the blackness and never awake, but connect with the
> ground, and shatter, watching myself die. Well, I'm on my way to
> Brooklyn, on my way to my death, or so it feels . . . I want to die, so
> I can finally go home. Home, a place where all my desires will . . .
> live.

Jill is beautiful, rich, and white, with a striking yet charming
bald haircut. She lives in California now. Her hair is starting to
grow out, and the stubble sprouts like the fruit on the farm where
she rides her horses. She makes her way around the land, doing
chores, in a scene of normal everyday life.

Shy and withdrawn, because life at home is difficult and trying, Jill says her father goes on rampaging drinking binges, shat-
tering the calm in the isolated woods, while her mother is unre-
tiring and vivacious. Jill has issues with her father.

In her journal, she writes of suicide as if it were a normal part
of teenage life:

I feel stranded with nowhere to go and if I want out of this world, where can I really go? All of the people around me make me want to cringe, to shrivel into a ball of emptiness. I want to disappear.

She then speaks of the suicide attempts:

I fall through the blackness and never awake, but connect with the ground, and shatter, watching myself die.

Or she writes of death and blood, matter-of-factly:

The first time was just for the blood. Me and Lauren decided the pentagon on my floor needed some of our blood to make it final. So we decided to scrape our skins with razor blades for some.

Jill tells me she became obsessed with death due to the fortune of her birth:

I was born dead. Yeah, I was born dead—blue, not breathing. Lucky for me, the nurse knew what she was doing, because there wasn't a doctor in sight. They cut my umbilical cord and I choked my way into this world. From that point on in life, I was pretty much quiet, observant, and shy. I don't really know why. Maybe I was just trying to understand this world and where I belonged in it.

Jill's suicidal thoughts and acts are no more bizarre than the bloodletting at some of the parties she attended. They have become like a rite of passage, a ritual one is bound to endure in order to be a teenager.

Jill's note is obscure and yet plain: "Well, I'm on my way to Brooklyn, on my way to my death, or so it feels . . . I want to die, so I can finally go home." It is almost as if she's writing a poem, as a way to tell someone, anyone who will listen, what she's feeling: that she is tired of living. The poem does have spiritual meaning, a kind of otherworldly pith in which she seeks to find solace, a place where she can be free.

The next day, this was where I found her, sitting against the school building wall, sunk in thought, her eyes vacant, her imagination raging. Maybe her thoughts race back to the family backyard and the swing she sat in as a child, reliving the story of the beautiful princess and the evil, haggard witch her parents told her about. But this reverie is broken as she writes in her journal about a sadness she can't quite heal:

> As a kid I was quiet and withdrawn from the beginning. To speak the truth, people just plain scared me silent. I'm not sure where my quietness came from except maybe my parents' outgoingness frightened me. My parents, quite frankly, scare me, and I swear, cross my soul and hope to die, I will never be their immortality.

She speaks to me to avoid hurting or betraying her parents, and her reluctance to speak makes it difficult to get at why she so often wrote about committing suicide.

> I think every decision that a child makes is rooted in the parents. I'm not saying that every time a kid commits suicide that it's the parents' fault. Let me get that straight. I'm saying that when a parent boxes a child in or doesn't let her or him make any decision on her own, that's when a kid wants to commit suicide.

Jill's father is a big man with rough hands who dresses like an executive, in a suit and tie, but covers the suit with starched gray overalls snapped up to the chest. He speaks in a kindly, business-man-like tone, confident and friendly.

Dad is a disciplinarian. He's always the one who set the day for everybody—my mom, me, and my sister and little brother. He tells me what he expects me to do every day, when to be home, how much homework has to be done, who to stay away from, and all of that. When I was a kid, if I didn't drink my milk he would ground me for a month. I couldn't leave the table until I drank my milk. My father wasn't exactly my best friend when I was in high school, and he would yell at me until I swallowed every drop. It would make me sick. One day, at school, they found out that I was lactose intolerant and milk made me sick. He refused to believe it and wanted to see the report and talk to the nurse. Instead of him being understanding and admitting he made a mistake on this, he said sometimes these tests can be wrong and perhaps we could find some kind of milk substitute.

Jill not only felt boxed in but also repeatedly gave her parents signs that she felt hemmed in—by too many rules, on the one hand, and by total inattention, on the other. And because such signals were ignored by her parents, Jill felt the need to replay her self-destructive acts over and over again.

I could have broken up with my boyfriend and shot myself in the head and it would still have something to do with my parents, because maybe I didn't feel my relationship with my parents was open enough that I could talk to them about it.

I would have felt trapped and too claustrophobic to ever mention I had a boyfriend to them.

You know, it's the whole Romeo and Juliet scenario. There's no place for the child to move without feeling that somehow the parents will reject them.

She spoke little about her alcoholic father, never convicting him, even in her diary, of wrongdoing. Quite the contrary, she forgave him for every early abuse. "I understand my father now, and though I hated him for what he did to me then, I don't feel that way now."

Girls with alcoholic or drug-abusing fathers often will experience some kind of unwanted touching, petting, kissing, or other sexual contact. Boys experience aggressive action from both parents, in the form of physical abuse, beatings, and verbal aggression. Fathers are usually the cause of anxiety in children because the father's role is more likely to be disciplinarian.[1]

Jill is clear when she says:

I tried to kill myself twice, once by not eating and once by bleeding to death. I just wanted the blood to make me go into shock and die. I would wear these baggy clothes, but my teachers noticed how skinny I was and they told my parents I was anorexic. The night I cut myself real deep, my friend bandaged me and I stayed over at her place. And around that time my mom saw the cuttings and made me see a therapist.

My mom is a manic person, and she is nothing but movement all the time, moving and fixing up the house, cleaning and stuff. She has a lot of energy. And so when she slows down, something is wrong. But nobody wants to have a relationship with their parents at seventeen. I'm sorry, but I certainly didn't. Anyway, after my mom found out about the cutting thing she told me I had to deal with it because she couldn't. She told me I had to get help.

Jill's mother is a wiry woman with red hair and bright green eyes. She dresses in tight jeans, talks a lot, and is quick in her actions. Jill describes the walk through the split-level house from her room to the other side, where her parents' rooms are located. The space is separated by a wide, modern, well-scrubbed kitchen and dining room. She points out that the garage area, which is several yards away from the house, is occupied by four cars and two trucks, parked haphazardly. Her father paints cars for a living—or at least decorates fine cars and trucks for customers. Jill calls it "exotic detailing."

My mother was pretty passive woman most of the time, and she would have a drink every now and then, and that would give her a little "Dutch courage" to challenge my father, but other than that she would just "get along to go along," as they say. I remember one time she told me never marry a man who beat me, and I asked her why she said that, and I didn't notice it then, but later I noticed her bruises. One day it would be on her arm; another time it would be on her face. But I was too young to really question what was happening or to even pay that much attention.

Jill didn't see a connection between the actions of her alcoholic father and her suicide attempts, because for her they were not cause and effect. She didn't see the gloom she was experiencing as part of something hidden deep inside of her head, surfacing as her anxiety-ridden life.

Kids are not always able to attack, blame, or confront parents at such tender ages, and the anxieties build to the point of needing release. That's when they begin to think of suicide as their only way out. Yet the path to suicide is a process. It begins in steps and is not one grand end-it-all event. For Jill, as for many others, it began with cutting.

The first year of junior high, I started cutting myself. I was about thirteen and a half years old. When I got to secondary school—and it was located in a one-room schoolhouse with a single teacher—I went to the bathroom one day and cut my leg. I had so much built up inside of me, it made me feel really alive. I would look into the mirror and see myself, and what I would see was not me. I didn't feel I was really me until I cut myself.

I had a situation where I would cut myself just to feel like there was a person underneath the skin. When I would see the blood, that's when I knew. I felt no pain when I cut myself.

It was not the first time I'd heard about kids who hurt themselves but felt nothing, but I wanted to know more about why this happened to Jill. Was there something in her personal experience that made her oblivious to pain—a trauma of some kind—or was it purely physical?

As a matter of fact, one day I was outside and I cut myself accidentally. Blood was running down my arm, and when I went into the building, a girl said, "Hey look, your arm is bleeding." And when I looked, it was at the opposite arm, because I couldn't feel it. And the cut was pretty deep.

I asked about her parents.

I didn't get along very well with my parents. My parents thought I was pretty difficult.

I have always had hair issues with my parents. I never had a haircut or color that my parents didn't hate. When I had my hair in dreads, they didn't like it. When I had my hair colored purple, they didn't like it. When I had orange knotted braids, they didn't like it. So when I shaved my head, they didn't like it very much, but it was my head and I did what I wanted. I had my head shaved in high school, and I was different. But because I was not very social I was a loner most of my high school years.

When Jill turned sixteen and had been cutting herself for about three years, her parents finally found out.

I wore pants all the time, and none of my cuts were visible. One day I was about to take a shower, and usually when I did I would always either put on a robe when I went to the bathroom or use two sets of towels. I'd wrap one towel around my legs and another one around my top.

But this time I went to the bathroom without thinking and didn't wrap my legs. I remember this was after I had gotten a tan, and my legs were all cut and the wounds were open and raw looking, and my mother happened to see me coming out of the bathroom and she freaked out.

Her mother asked what happened.

I told her. But you gotta understand my mom. If you had a nose-
bleed, she'd freak. She is such a wuss. But I cut myself all through
high school.

I put a lot of this in my journals. I started writing because I was
not very social and I had so much inside of me that it was the best
place for me to let go. It helped me feel a release as well.

I looked it up and did some more research on cutting to try
and understand what I was doing to myself. And I learned that
there is something in the brain, this adrenaline, that makes the
pain minimal or not at all . . . That explains why it hurt some people to cut themselves and doesn't hurt others. I wanted to know
why people cut themselves, too.

Jill is about cutting and suicide—and, in a sense, the neuro-
science of cutting, if there is such a thing—but there is confusion about the relationship between scarring surfaces of the body
(without being aware that one might die) and killing the body. In
other words, cutting and scarring the body may be seen as an un-
conscious suicide attempt on her part. My sense, however, is that
Jill's cutting was actually a morbid form of self-healing, because
the suicidal impulse she experienced was focused on a part of her
body (her legs) rather than on her whole body.

This raises the issue of body image in relation to scarring: the
scar is always there as a reminder. Unable to find a healing solution to the childhood pains and traumas that build up inside
them, many kids begin to cut, choke, or bind themselves. These
acts offer a kind of self-medicating release of the inner problems

they feel they have no other way of expressing. It creates a physical manifestation, such as a scar or a blue mark, of a pain they often can't identify, and it presents a warning sign for parents and friends that something is wrong. Like a drug, all forms of self-mutilation enable the victim to focus on something other than her or his own life, and although not all such actions are precursors to suicide, they are all extremely dangerous—a major artery may be accidentally cut, or a binding and choking method may result in blackout, coma, or death.

One in every two hundred kids (mostly girls) is involved in secret cutting rituals; that amounts to about two million kids a year in the United States. When these kids do cut themselves, as Jill did for a number of years, the purpose is to relieve the built-up tension they feel inside, and to manifest the pain.[2] They like to see the blood because, as Jill put it, "It puts me into a calm state." Although Jill wanted to understand how much pain she could endure, she also cut herself for the thrill of it. That is, the cuts weren't always about wanting to die (although that could happen accidentally) but about the excitement of knowing that, when the blood begins to flow, she is alive.

When I asked her why she made cuts on her thighs, she replied, "Because that is where I get fat." When I inquired at a New York psychiatric facility about cases like Jill's, a counselor said, "Cutting, anorexia, and bulimia are also manifestations, probably 90 percent of the time, of early childhood sexual abuse. So with this form of self-mutilation, you would say they're hurting themselves in specific places for some specific reason. And that reason is usually because, in one way or another, they have a distorted body image and hate their bodies in general." Based on this assessment, then, most of the kids presented here as cutters would be victims of sexual abuse.

Friends of Jill's confirmed that her shaved head and the cutting were related to her suicide attempts and were a form of self-disgust. I felt the issues went deeper, to questions about self-image and perhaps even to sexual abuse, but those close to Jill held other opinions. One friend said:

> Well, I think it has to do with how she felt about her body. She was upset about the way she looked, and her weight, even though she was not overweight or anything. She was just one of those strong, horse-riding farm girls. I saw the cuttings on her legs one day when we went swimming at a place called the Devil's Gorge. I saw the cuts all over her legs when she was about to jump off the bank. She looked at me and I looked at her, and at that moment, we both had this secret. But we didn't talk to each other about it until one night about a year later, when I stayed over at her house.
>
> She said it was a real relief to talk about it. I was very shaken by what she told me. The next day I made the cardinal sin of telling my mom, even though Jill told me not to tell anyone. I told my mom because she told me she wouldn't say anything. But she let Jill's mom know, by asking her to read an article about cutting. And though Jill denied it, her mom, sometime later, saw cuts on her legs, too. After that, Jill's mom threatened to send her to a psychiatrist and have these doctors examine her, and it scared Jill so much she stopped cutting herself for a while.

When parents are not sure how to deal with the problems of a child, they often threaten the child with everything from religion to psychotherapy. In most cases, these methods could be more helpful to their kids than doing nothing at all; everyone needs someone to talk to who will listen to them objectively and without prejudice. But if a counselor or doctor is acting solely on behalf of the parent who pays or contacts them, then trust is immediately destroyed—for that encounter and for future ones. When this happens, the act itself is negated and the child suffers because it becomes harder to trust the parent or anyone else who says they want to help. At the same time, I believe an adolescent must be given the power, as it were, to seek a psychotherapist, though of course most minors do not have such power or privilege. In most cases, this should be a joint venture, undertaken by parent and child in unison, when the child is ready.

In the town there was this man who all the kids sorta hung out at his house. He was independently wealthy, I guess you could say, and he liked all the kids, and was into astronomy and spiritualist stuff. One day I went there and he had two girls handcuffed together, and I thought that was weird, but they wanted to be locked together and he let them. He was a painter, too, and I was infatuated with him. We never had anything sexual going on, but I would visit him and he'd talk to me and introduce me to books and literature and stuff like that. He had these animals he loved— birds and cats and rabbits and stuff all in cages. He was like a pied piper of sorts. Of course, when my parents found out I was going there, they stopped me. Especially my dad, who was very upset and told me never to go there again.

Since Jill's mother knew about the cutting but not about the male stranger, Jill felt she had an outlet, though not a physical, sexual one. But once her parents found out about the stranger, some kind of professional intervention should not have been a threat but a promise. Jill didn't receive psychiatric help, and the cutting didn't stop. Instead, the situation worsened into a serious blood ritual.

After the thing with my mother finding out about my cuts, I was very upset and tense for a long time. And I hadn't cut myself for months. So I went up to my room one day and started cutting my legs again. Just as I did that, my brother almost caught me. I freaked. Then I called my friend over, because I was trying to cut deeper now, trying to get the pain out that was all built up. I wanted her there just in case something went wrong.

When her friend arrived, she found Jill crouched in the corner of her room holding an odd-colored cloth. On closer inspection, she saw that it was a bloodstained rag. "I asked Jill what it was," her friend remembers, "and she said it was her cutting rag that had become her reminder of past hurt. It was like an heirloom or something."

Her friend, at that instant, became part of Jill's secret ritual, and because the rag had been with Jill since her first cut, it was like an addict's needle or a crackhead's pipe—an instrument with a history, a keepsake, a reminder of her past and her present. It was a valued object that reminded her of the times she was alive. This is another example of suicidal teenagers and their shared network of feelings, and Jill's friend was part of that network.

Jill told me:

Back then, it was really something unusual (cutting and shaved heads), especially for a girl. The kids who did this were considered strange and with real problems, but now the kids do it just to be cool. It's not the same. I didn't hate my body; I just wanted to feel alive. And I didn't unless I cut myself.

Underneath the pain, Jill and these other young people feel, are the deeper causes of their anxiety, a worry couched in secrecy about why they feel the way they do and why they cannot divulge the source of their problem.

> Society is basically phony. The parents of all my friends have let them down. The teachers of all my friends have let them down. So I'd rather live my life the way I want, without anybody telling me what the fuck to do, because ain't nobody out there that I trust but myself.

Parents play a much larger role in the suicide of their children than they realize. They often walk a tightrope between getting too close to their kids and pushing their kids away, between asking too many questions and asking too few. In the end, most end up alienating their kids even more. If parents pay too little attention, the kids hate them for not caring, and if they pay too much attention, the kids think they are meddlesome. Other parents push their kids to succeed, and that can be a problem as well. There is no one right answer and, unfortunately, there are no training schools for parenting, so parents are left to figure out for themselves how to relate to every child as an individual with his or her own quite individual needs. It is a daunting task.

> My dad was worried about me being abused, and when I think about it, we all may have been abused. I mean, there are varying degrees of abuse, and it depends on how you react to the particular situation. For example, if you got an uncle who wants a kiss from you, whether you want to kiss him or not, that may be abuse, because he's getting off on that kiss, and you don't know it yet but you are developing disgust about kissing anyone. You could be developing a fetish for older men, or some other factor in your sexuality, based on those experiences. I think it depends on how

sensitive the child is. I know I started to care more about horses than people after a while, and it may have been because this man cared for animals and I cared for him and I was told to avoid him, which created an attachment or a longing.

Jill completed her course at a hairstylist institute and lives at home with her horses. She feels that the years of tension around who she was then, with all the cutting, bulimia, and suicide attempts, were a phase that changed her life. It is certainly the case with Jill that these suicidal ideations were a phase of her life, and one reason she evolved was that she moved away from her parents' home. This was a step toward redemption, in many ways, and it shows how a person can transition away from suicidal feelings. There is also a bit of mystery about how this kind of sustained therapeutic process works. It certainly does not work for everyone.

I've always said that I needed to go through those things in order to be where I am today. I would not have lived my life any differently if I had to do it all over again. I'm stronger, wiser, and more in tune with my inner self now, after that experience. I'm a much better person, and I know I can help my kids, when they grow up, to be better human beings, as a result of what I've gone through as a woman-child.

9

ON THE ROAD

Cody

Cody is eighteen years old and has recently decided to go on the
road.

> I'm not sorry that I did this. I don't have reason to be. I can no
> longer endure the pain. Life is abuse. I have felt suffocated for too
> long. I have been taught to be ashamed for thinking and for feel-
> ing. It is not even possible for me to control my own life anymore.
> My control has been auctioned off to some omnipotent force that
> I'm afraid we have created.
>
> I can't stand facing what we are and what we have made. Yes,
> cancer and garbage disposals will get you. Yes, the world is a ter-
> rible place, yes, a war is coming, the world shot to hell and you're
> all goners. Your fear, your own lives are your entertainment. I just
> need to turn it off. One can only hold on for so long before letting
> go. We have strayed so far and I can't find my way back.
> Cody
> p.s. hopefully work will allow you to take a day off for my burial.

Cody is a short, wiry white kid, who looks a lot younger than
his years. His narrow face is unscarred, though a small amount of

peach fuzz, as he calls it, grows on his chin. His hands are fragile, the fingers short, the nails bitten low. There is a lone, newly etched tattoo of a phoenix rising on the underside of his right wrist.

Cody's suicide note is cathartic. It is the culmination of many events. However, the postscript is telling. It more than suggests that Cody feels like an afterthought, that his parents' careers take precedence. In other words, he is not even important when dead.

When he could not take the stress, the beatings, the screaming, he wrote a suicide note to his father. This note above was left for his family one day after his father refused to take time off work to come to Cody's school. Cody explains:

> I wrote that note out of respect for my loved ones, because I wanted my parents to have some peace of mind, in a way, so they would know why I killed myself. I thought that my note would be a way of sharing my feelings, because I felt ashamed, and feeling ashamed is really a weakness. I think, in another way, the note is my last way of blaming those who had not tried to understand me and who did not try to understand my viewpoint.

Shame should not be seen as a weakness; a feeling, act, or experience that brings about strong regret is not entirely a bad thing. Kids need to and do feel the importance of regretting their actions, and this reveals strength, not weakness. The courage to admit that one feels ashamed is an indication of strength, or a display of strength.

But Cody was taught to be ashamed when he exhibited or showed certain emotions, and he was chastised for such expression.

> My dad would tell me not to act this way or that way because boys don't act that way. He would say, "Little boys don't feel that way; be

a man, don't cry, and don't show that side of yourself. You're crying; you should be ashamed." He always said showing feelings was bad.

There is evidence here of an intergenerational conceptualization about emotions and what it means to be a man; whenever Cody showed his emotions (as a man should), he was taught to feel ashamed. But Cody's situation with his father goes much deeper, and it began early.

My dad and me got along until I was about seven, and then one day he just hauled off and started beating me for something I didn't do. Ever since then, we only get along for like a week or two at a time before we get into another fight. I think one of the reasons we don't get along now is that we are both very stubborn. I think the other thing is he's just a really bitter person.

That's how I can describe him. Once something bad happens, he's bitter about it for a real long time and he can't let it go. And at this point, after all the arguments—physical fights—I just don't think it's meant for us to like each other. I don't think that there's anything available there, and one of those things [that's missing] is a relationship. I really feel it's one of them things in life. There's just some people—even though he is my blood, he's my father— there are people in this world that you can't get along with. I think he's one of them. Honestly.

The anger and resentment, built up over years of abuse, culminated in Cody stabbing his father.

He asked me a question about where I had been, and I mumbled under my breath, and he said I cursed at him. He started hitting me, and I couldn't take that shit no more, so I grabbed a steak knife and cut him. We wrestled and I got away and ran over to my friend's house.

Two nights after the police came looking for him at his friend's house, Cody was caught setting fire to a local warehouse, and although the court delayed the hearing on the incident for several months, Cody decided to leave home and never return.

The fire was not set deliberately. I don't care what my mom told you. I was running away and went to hide behind this building. It got cold and I lit a fire. When some wood caught fire next to where I was laying, I just didn't put it out. I told the judge this, but he didn't believe me.

Cody said the incident with his dad changed him. After years of beatings and humiliation, now all Cody thought about was ways to commit suicide. He also knew, after this incident, that he couldn't live at home and feel safe anymore. When Cody went to his friend's house, all bloody, after stabbing the father who had beaten him:

I was gonna shoot myself. I had the gun. I had the bullets, and I put one round in the chamber, put it to my head, but didn't pull the trigger. Something told me to do it, and then I heard this other voice telling me not to.

This was not the first time Cody attempted suicide; in fact, it started long before.

I first tried to kill myself when I was eight. I was supposed to have a babysitter coming over that night because my parents were going out. The babysitter called to say she would be a little late, so my parents left before she got there.

I went into the kitchen drawer and got this rope, wrapped it around my neck, and we had this window above the door, which slanted out, and I threw the rope in between there and stood on a chair. And as I was standing there, trying to get my feet straight, the babysitter walked in and started screaming.

She talked to me for a little bit and got really nervous and called my parents. After that, my parents called in a psychiatrist and I started seeing him for a while.

In high school, Cody tried to kill himself using inhalants, which he insists were powerful enough to "kill a horse."

I was inhaling air dusters [used to clean computer equipment], and on more than one occasion. And I climbed up on this really highway overpass one day and thought about jumping. If it wasn't for my friends, I'd be dead by now.

I never had a suicide date or plan or stuff like that, but I would try and kill myself when things got really shitty and I would really feel like it. What would push me to the edge would be when I'd get into arguments with my dad and all those times I would feel lonely. That was when I would go to a tall building and think about jumping, or get my dad's gun.

He still has a recurring dream in which he dies when the gun goes off. He wakes up thinking he's actually dead. "I've had these dreams for a long time, and I think that's because I came so close to killing myself."

The most serious suicide attempt was with a gun his father kept under the bed.

One day my friend was there with me, and I put the bullet in, and we were in the backyard. And he said, "No, don't put it to your head. Just see if you would be dead or not. Pull the trigger." And when I pulled the trigger, the bullet shot straight in the air.

I dropped the gun and we just sat down on the grass, and I was so nervous. I was shaking. I jumped up after that and put the gun away. I didn't do that anymore.

Cody grew closer to his friends after this incident, and he put more faith in them, though he did not stop his suicidal ways. We have seen this network of shared feelings with friends in the lives of some of the other kids in this book.

Cody pauses to consider what he's about to say, and then tells me:

Suicide is an escape from a hurtful place. I sought suicide because the world is a painful place for me. I see and feel the world as painful. The pain didn't end, and neither did my attempts to escape it.

Today, Cody looks like a runaway. His head is wrapped in a calico sweatband and he is wearing a black T-shirt advertising the heavy metal band Neurosis. His once-blue overalls now have large, colorful patches. They are cut off at the knee and resewn around the edges. The blue color, darkened by wear, has an oily, heavily worn patina, a slickness that leaves a permanent crease across the material. His sneakers, like his pants, are well worn. His hair, dark with a slightly brownish tint, is styled in a spiky punk crew cut, and his eyebrows are thick and brown. A pointing-arrow tattoo across the bridge of his nose gives him a calm, peaceful look. He has soft, wide-set eyes, and his lips favor a smile rather than a sneer.

Cody is talkative as he rests his foot on a brick wall, rolling a cigarette. He's reflecting on his life and the people in it, talking about his most recent trip. He's decided to run away again because of the treatment he gets at home. Running—like cutting, drug taking, shooting, or hanging—is a solution to an intolerable situation. It is the way he relieves his inner pain, a self-medication that helps protect him from the past while he avoids a future. But Cody is trying to find himself, too, and like so many other kids, his approach is unique.

I think, for a kid, everything that happens to them, whether it's craziness, suicide, drug use, racism, it starts at home, with the family. You know, your mother and your father are the ones who do the most good or the most damage to you as a kid. And then, after a while, after the parents have fucked up, kids then start to only listen to other kids, especially nowadays.

They don't listen to their parents anymore, because they have listened to their parents all their lives and all they learned was fucked-up shit. Then one day they discover that their world is really with other kids, and that's the world they have to survive in, not home. But the parents don't understand that world, and eventually they misunderstand their kids, and the kids begin to drift. And the parents give up.

So the parents have to learn all over again about their own kids, mostly after it's too late. You know, most parents would rather let their kids struggle with life rather than change their own way of seeing stuff.

In some ways, kids today live in a virtual world half the time. Kids have their computers and games and the Internet, and their parents can't even enter those worlds without the kid's permission, though it is not only technology that creates virtual worlds for kids, and certainly it is not impossible for parents to enter these worlds as well.

This year (1999), Cody, like so many kids today, used the Internet. This makes kids feel they are in control, and they like it. So, many parents are there as providers but really nothing more. To keep a kid safe and straight these days, parents have to be, as Cody noted, "not just good [parents], but real lucky."

Cody's modes of transport are hitchhiking and hopping railroad cars, a particularly dangerous adventure in which many young people die every year. In this way, he relieves himself of certain demons by taking other, more precarious risks.

> The road definitely calls my name a lot. I think life should be fun now because I have not had a lot of fun in my life. I like the challenge of traveling, hitchhiking, because I like the idea of, like, you can drop me off anywhere in the United States and I'll be fine. But I know that hitchhiking is like conquering the fear of death.
>
> I guess I was running away from my father, or at least from my family. I might have been running away from myself, too, I guess.

Without much prompting, Cody tells me about a dark family legacy. "I really wasn't told about the family suicides as a little boy," he says, looking over at me sheepishly. This reference to a "crazy gene" underscores the idea of intergenerational trauma and raises questions about what happens when suicide occurs from one generation to the next. The big question here is whether mental illness runs in Cody's family and whether it has been passed on to the next generation. Will Cody commit suicide like so many in his family? Will he survive the crazy gene? He articulates this matter with some concern.

Cody's face and body are like a text, something to read, to study for clues. The small beard of facial hair he acquired on the road makes him look younger, not older, even though the peach fuzz is slightly thicker now. He waxes philosophical.

It seems I've always been running away, from one thing or another, all my life. It was only when I was older that I found out about the three folks on my dad's side who killed themselves. My whole family on my dad's side basically went crazy—like schizophrenic crazy—or committed suicide. I'm as normal as any of the kids I grew up with, but I qualify that by saying my childhood was also a little weird because of the shit I took from my father. I guess I had a normal childhood, as far as what "normal" could be. Also, I guess it was normal compared to what happened to some of my friends, with the rapes, incest, beatings, and stuff, and all kinds of other psychological and physical abuse they took.

Cody's suicide attempts, and his decision to hitchhike and to expose himself to new dangers, in an unknown world, were his way of trying to overcome the anxieties about his past experiences. Maybe he was just running away from his current set of problems, or perhaps he was more consciously or intentionally escaping, knowing that it might be dangerous and that he might be killed on the road.

The trip, he thought, would be an awakening. He knew he had to come back, at some point, to face both his family and one issue in particular: the arson charge, a situation that had hung over him since his junior year of high school. In the letters and postcards he sent to me, I could see him gaining the maturity to come back to deal with this problem. The travels made him see himself in a whole new way, and though it might not have solved all of his problems, it did relieve the most immediate aggravation, which was life at home. Running away from home, he said, was one of the few options he had.

> I didn't have money to rent an apartment, and I didn't have a job in the town. A lot of people thought I was a troublemaker because of the fire I set, and plus I was suffocating in that place. What I wanted to do was get out of the town that hated me, and away from a family that hated me. Although I should say *my dad*, because my mom didn't want me to leave.

Cody needed to get out of town because he, like so many of the other kids chronicled here, had a strong need to invent or reinvent himself. Street socialization, another idea that runs through the heart of all these teen notes, also can be viewed as a refusal to accept the adult cultural model. Kids hang out with other kids, who provide support and assist them in surviving in what can be a tough and dangerous world. These kids are not learning or getting their social skills from the locations most acceptable in the society (family and school) but from other adolescents, in the street.

Cody wasn't prepared to travel, because he had little money, but he was determined to go across the United States to visit friends in California. Over the next few months, he wrote letters and postcards to me and to friends, from the road. In one, he said, "But all I needed to go was the courage, a thumb, and a bag on my back."

The troubles he was about to face were perhaps not as overpowering as his past troubles—his family, the humiliation, and the psychic pain that he endured. Cody felt that if he stayed in that town, in that house, in that family, he would die. He had no choice but to get away. But running away, hitchhiking with strangers, riding on lightless boxcars, sleeping in deserted parks and under highway embankments may be tantamount to suicide, because the risks, though different, are just as scary.

If he learns something, though, this may be the better option. Suicide seemed a viable option when Cody left home, but, luckily for him, he did learn something: perspective. When kids are wrapped up in their everyday lives—when they are fighting with their families, when school is a drag, or when there are no real friends around to help them out—the world can be a very bleak place. Because they often feel that the weight of the world is on their shoulders, every teenager can use a little perspective to help them move out from underneath that weight and see things for what they really are. Staring into the ocean, peering through a telescope, or simply taking a long walk through the park or around the block and looking at everything around can show us that the world is a lot greater and more complex than even our worst secrets and fears. Keeping this in mind, and experiencing these things firsthand, can help anyone clear their head, so they can make more rational and intelligent decisions about their lives.

There is a distinction between leaving home and running away. Leaving home is a choice, made without pressure from one's family, and is not necessarily a rejection of middle-class or family values. Kids leave home for many reasons, including a desire for adventure, ideological sagacity, or because it makes disordered good sense. The action could, in fact, be viewed as a kind of "kid power," or at least behavior that is not unconventional at all. Running away, on the other hand, suggests, by its very name, an act of rebellion, an active choice on the part of the kid.

And although this is true as received wisdom, the internal logic—revelations by letter or journal of attempted suicide—has to be understood at psychological face value in order to have meaning. Households and family structures can be wonderful or truly rotten places for children and teenagers—emotionally and psychologically—and it is clear from Cody's commentary that the real danger of being a child or a teenager is just that: being a child or a teenager, and thus being dependent and having nowhere to go.

> I wanted to kill myself, to give up, like a lot of other kids do, and take the easy way out. But a lot of kids are lost, too, and have some misplaced aggression, and they end up killing others as well. Listen, if I stay for two days with my parents, I'm crazy already. They make me crazy. Bottom line. I know a lot of kids feel the same way. We need to escape from our parents—not forever, just for a long time—and then come back at a later time.

There is no mention here of running to extended family—grandparents, uncles, or aunts—because I do not think Cody felt there were other familial safe havens. This does not strike me as odd, because he desires to extricate himself from his family, and that means *all* of his family, and because he has issues with intergenerational trauma raising its ugly head in his extended family. In the end, children and teenagers trust their peers and look to them for support, if not guidance. Parents and adults become the Other and, if you will, the enemy.

What happens when the beauty that exists in the world does not reach people who have been damaged? Are despair, loneliness, and suicidal rages legitimate emotions that are part and parcel of the human experience? The one major idea that I have grasped from Cody's narrative and others is the isolation of children, and their invisibility, which contributes greatly to their abuse and maltreatment. Furthermore, what does child-rearing mean? It is not a uniform practice across cultures and ethnic backgrounds. Adrian Peterson, a football player for the Minnesota Vikings, beat his son with a "switch" (a tree branch), and to him this was culturally normative. State authorities, however, viewed this action as constituting child abuse.

Cody's letters from the road provide answers to some of those questions. Each reveals something about himself: wisdom, some new knowledge about a different culture, a shattered stereotype. He's traveling to avoid the past and to get perspective on his future.

In one letter, he asks whether he is courageous and wonders how he can adjust to the world and see people differently. He wants to know how he can escape the racism of his father. Cody is driven by this curiosity, this quest, this chance event, and by trying to not repeat the mistakes of his past. "I think life's greatest adventures are the ones you put your life on the line for. And I don't think this is a self-destructive behavior at all."

Ironically, when Cody got to the West Coast, he found that one of his friends was in the hospital after a suicide attempt. Cody's reaction is provocative and protective in a way that is surprising, because he gets angry:

> I got angry because he's basically giving up, letting go. But, at the same time, I understand. The things that helped me was, first, music, then my friends, and finally traveling. As far as music goes, I just get relaxed when I listen to music, and my friends help because they are there. It's not even by talking directly about my problems but just hanging around them. You see, living is hard and painful, and it's easy to kill yourself, although that's a blunt way of putting it.

I used to see life as a painful place, and I still do, but it has a lot beauty, too. I no longer see suicide as an option as I once did, because of my experiences traveling, because I see life so much more differently now.

Cody's travel daring is his way of not committing suicide, and although it is still a borderline physical risk, it also is a quest for adventure. Therefore, the action, this traveling and moving out of a place that is confining to his emotional well-being, is basically about reinvention.

A lot of my problems were internal, about my blaming myself, because they were things I needed to work out and didn't or couldn't. I think any kid who has any trace of mental problems at all, those problems—unless it's some chemical imbalance—have to be connected to their environment.

I believe he means here the social environment at large. Cody decided to leave home because he felt he had to find some answers, and maybe those answers would help him cope with his dilemma. He didn't want to die until he had found those answers. But running away isn't too far from holding a gun to your head, because the risks and dangers are vast, and if he runs, he doesn't have to make a decision about death. It's open, and if he dies . . . well, that's what he wanted anyway.

Last year, Cody placed an ad in local newspaper, seeking work as a blacksmith's apprentice, and got three responses.

Two didn't work out for various reasons, but a third one, in New Jersey, worked out fine. I get to live there free room and board, and

I get to learn this skill, which is what I wanted. I don't get paid, so all I need to do is get some pocket money. As far as the suicide thing goes, I've moved beyond that now. I have lots of friends here. I keep myself busy, which helps a lot, too. I don't have time to be thinking about negative things. I have a nice relationship with my dad, too. I was happy when I was traveling, but this is different. I'm happy where I am right now.

Cody makes a lot of very interesting observations. One of the key ideas, though, as it relates to the end of Cody's narrative, is the need to leave his parents' home and, by proxy, the community. I interpret this as a "solution" to suicidal ideation—or at least Cody's solution.

Overall, I think life can be painful, because we have to go through a lot of trials, and that's the reason why kids want to kill themselves. They want to turn life off because they don't wanna deal with it. But now I know that if you live long enough you go through everything, and nothing is so bad if you can wake up the next day and face it.

10

BORN-AGAIN VIRGIN

Gabriella

Gabriella was seventeen and a half when I met her, and she had a lot to say:

> I wanted to jump, but I knew it would be messy, so I didn't. The second time I was gonna jump and told myself to call him and if he didn't answer I would kill myself. But he answered the phone and we ended up talking for two hours and I went to sleep after that.

Gabriella had been depressed since she got pregnant and, for her, suicide represented relief from a bad, regrettable situation: "I got pregnant because he was careless and I was stupid."

In her frazzled state, she wrote to the father of her baby:

> Dear you:
>
> I saw you in a different light tonight. In my head it made sense, just as it always seems to, but when I step back, I realize that I build my castle in the sand. You're not even close to the person I want to be with, but still, I get angry. My feelings are so erratic with you—your

immaturity, your murky intentions, your sex ambivalent. I wanted
to tell you this a few days ago. You were just here on Thursday.
Wanted to tell then but had to pull my thoughts together. You're in
my way, of doing the things I should, of being the person I could,
of moving higher.

Gabriella's story is about suicide as a solution to an irresolvable conflict in which she has become trapped between what her parents have taught her and what her own heart is telling her. She has to choose between the preaching, admonitions, and values of her mother and her own feeling for a boy, which has put her in an impossible situation.

Barely five feet tall, weighing no more than ninety pounds, Gabriella is a bleach blond with a butch-femme look. She wears hip-hugging jeans that reveal a heart-shaped tattoo around her navel, and black combat boots. Her articulate and sophisticated manner reveals a well-read and experienced teenager. Her charming sensuality and natural beauty give her an air of innocence, though her conversation quickly makes it clear that she is hardly innocent.

I became interested in writing her story when I learned that she kept diaries in which she had written about cutting. She was one of Megan's "family" (chapter 3), the friend of a friend who told me about this "fantastic girl" who loved to dance and knew about the Goth scene in the city. This is a typical snowball effect: a circle of teenagers I had come to know talked to me about other teenagers who were talking about suicide.

I read through one section of Gabriella's diary and noticed a story about a recent suicide attempt, following a broken relationship with a boy. This was odd, since Gabriella is an avowed lesbian, but the details of this story make up this chapter. She wrote:

We're both gay. You're involved with someone different every month of the year, you don't approach the levels of honesty, sincerity, or good will that I need. I saw you tonight with your flavor of your month companion, and you seemed affectionate, concerned.

Gabriella explains:

I've always hated men. When people ask me why or how, I'd explain that it was like a gift I got at birth. Some people can sing; others can dance. I was blessed with the innate gift of hating men. My gift gave me a vision through which I could see right through the sniveling, unwavering face of even the most well-meaning man. I never questioned the goodwill of my opinions.

Gabriella calls herself a "born-again virgin" because she decided to stop dating boys and to start dating girls, and now, in her late teens, she is confused and hurt, and interested in maybe getting married one day. The issues surrounding her attempted suicide led her to write in her diary:

Dear you:

. . . I can't imagine how this will end. But it will not be good. If I die from my own hands I hope you will know you played a major role in it. I can't go on like this.

I knew from Gabriella's journal that her mother, father, grandmother, and aunts played a larger-than-life role in her sexual orientation and were the source of love as well as of resentment and much distress. Once again, family life represents an emotional and cultural transmission center for intergenerational trauma.

"My mother raised me, mostly, but basically I was brought up in a house full of women, including my maternal grandmother, and they were all man-haters." I asked her why they were man-haters and she ignored the question, saying, "I'll get to that."

You see, I was raised by nunlike women in a strictly heterosexual, male-dominated family. My mother was always there for me, just like she is now.

And my grandmother lived there with us, and I would usually spend the day there with her. And I'd wake up and, if it was a weekend, I would go to dance class and then come back. What I'd do is wake up and go make breakfast and go back to my room and spend basically the entire day in my room, writing in my journal, talking to friends on the phone, go out to the mall later on.

Now, there was never any real family dinner or anything like that, though my grandmother would ask us to break bread once a week together. But somebody was always missing, either my father or one of the men living with my aunts. But we'd rarely be with each other, and I'd take the food to my room. My mother would be in and out all day and she really wouldn't talk; she'd just moan and groan.

We'd say, "Mom, how are you?" and she'd say, "Eh," or something like that. And then my father would come home at night and he'd knock on the door or something like that. He'd come home and knock on my door, just to let me and my sister know he was home, so we would acknowledge his presence—so that we could start stepping and fetchin' for him.

My mother was always in the kitchen, or cleaning up after us and my father. She was making food or something, along with all the other women in the house. You see, I lived with my aunts and grandmother, all of whom had men in the house, husbands who were little dictators, telling them and us what to do all the time. My mother would get up at five in the morning to make coffee and breakfast for my father, because he had to be at work by seven, and then she'd go back to sleep. My aunts, the same thing: always catering to them men.

My room was downstairs and looked completely different from the rest of the house. It was black and white, but I prefer to call it "champagne." And I had this bedroom set I had picked out myself, and I had a few posters from Broadway shows. I had a few pictures of friends, but it was pretty boring as well. I had some pages of magazines, of clothes I had found, that was all over the floor. It was definitely nothing.

My father would see me leaving the house and say I dressed like a slut or that I was acting slutty. Or that I looked like a whore. Am I the slut he wants to be with? Is he describing me? Or is he describing some character he wants me to be? Well, his comments weren't innocent words, because they went with touching me, and all of that made me think. He would say these things, these sexual words to me. I was at an age when I was becoming sexual, and because of him I also started to feel like I hated sexuality to a certain extent. I really believe I would have been heterosexual had I not had this experience with my father.

I know I developed this feeling, though I didn't know it at the time, that I wanted to have some power over this kind of experience, and that translated into having to overcome my fear of men and control what happened to me sexually. At fourteen, I had no power. I would just prance around in my tutu and he'd look with his lustful eyes at me and say those things to me. And I was his daughter; what could I do or say?

So this made me feel like, *One day, I'll have the power to turn this thing around.* In my life, I didn't have that many chances to assert my power. I didn't have any power, or at least at the time I didn't think I did. Any man, any boy, could do whatever they wanted to me and I couldn't do anything about it.

Gabriella desperately sought a solution to her problem but, finding no way out, chose suicide. I asked if she minded talking about these things and she assured me there was no issue at all. She wanted to talk, because nobody else, except a few close friends, had discussed these issues. "Anyhow, Megan told me about you, and I heard from Gita, too, that you be good people. You can ask me whatever you want."

I began by asking whether she had a suicide plan. She thinks for a moment and then, rolling her green eyes downward, says:

It wasn't so much a plan as much as it was a lot more spontaneous. I don't know if I actually told you, but we [she and her boyfriend] would go up on his roof and talk and smoke cigarettes. And it was then I thought about the beauty of doing it [jumping from the roof] up there. So it wasn't so planned out, but as I think about it, it was calculated to make him suffer by watching me die.

No matter what their parents might say, if kids instinctively feel different, they must learn to identify with that difference and to educate themselves. They must begin at an early age to search for some means of self-preservation. When warning signals go off in their heads, when someone says something they don't feel is right, when they're hit or abused, they should take note of those warnings. And when kids begin trusting themselves at an early age, listening to the warnings they give themselves, suicide will be replaced by survival.

The male-dominated family to which Gabriella refers was ruled by her father, who treated her with indifference and, in her words, "abused" her whenever he could. However, she then says that although it was "somewhat sexual," it was no big deal.

> Yes, he touched me, but it was not what you think. He did say I was the cause of it because I was a little tease, and for a long time I believed him, especially through junior high. He didn't want me to have any boyfriends then, and when I did show interest in boys, he'd spank me—even if I talked on the phone to boys.

This is a rationalization of the sexual abuse by her father, and it means that Gabriella is a bit disingenuous when she says she was born hating men. In a cursory way, what Gabriella says here reminds me of a profile in another book, in which a superintendent recounts what he sees/hears in terms of a father, or maybe a stepfather, having some sort of sexual relationship with his daughter/ stepdaughter.[1]

Gabriella's family house is located on a cul-de-sac, next to three other homes with nice lawn furniture and sprinkler systems. The cars square off in a semicircle around the driveway, and all are worker vehicles: a Chevrolet Impala, a Ford truck, and a Honda. The house seems small, with a large kitchen and a smallish living area, but this is only because two plastic-covered sofas, a middle table, two lamps, and three chairs give the room a busy feel. Though Gabriella's grandmother was too ill to come down from her room, her father came in and gave me a strong handshake before leaving for the city. Gabriella doesn't live at home anymore, but she pointed toward her old room, which is now occupied by her little sister.

Gabriella's mother, a diminutive woman with a striking face and round, expressive eyes, was graceful and open when speaking about her daughter, but surprisingly conservative, too. Our conversation was a mixed bag. When I broached the subject of teenage sexuality, Gabriella's mother quickly interjected. She sees herself as a liberated woman, and sex is something she felt free to discuss frankly. Gabriella had explained my research to her but had not said much about the present work on suicide. She said she was taking me to a Goth club. I was prepared to discuss the work I was doing, but no one asked about it yet.

I was intrigued that Gabriella's father just shook my hand and headed off to the city. Because I had heard so much about his place in this male-dominated household, this struck me as both curious and odd, until Gabriella explained that her father was estranged from his wife and was not living in the house at the time of my visit. Gabriella said he was "banished."

I think Gabriella's parents' ideas about "appropriate" behavior sowed the seeds for her confused sexual orientation. Her mother taught some conflicting values. On the one hand, she expected Gabriella to be sexually conservative, but on the other, Gabriella interpreted those lessons as a guide to sexual freedom, and that meant it was acceptable to experience sex with girls. I believe Gabriella was as much a contrarian as one can be and that she rebelled against the conservative values of her mother by interpreting them as a kind of freedom. Gabriella specifically interpreted those lessons to mean "do the exact opposite." Her mother later said she wanted grandchildren. I thought perhaps Gabriella would tell me how her father's inappropriate touching and spanking during her adolescent years was the basis of her hatred of boys, and why she turned to girls, but it was more than that.

When Gabriella had invited me to the family home, she said her mother would like to meet me (though she said nothing about her father). She had told her mother I was writing about teenagers and had written other books, and she had showed her mother the book I had written with William Kornblum, *Growing Up Poor*. Her mother said she had heard about some of my books but had not read them. (I think she was just being kind.) I explained more about what I was doing presently, writing about kids and suicide.

I glanced over at Gabriella. Her lips formed a tiny smirk and she winked as her mother told me more about her sexual beliefs, and why kids have no reason to be thinking about suicide, and that it's the parents' fault if a kid kills herself. She asked me why I was writing about suicide and not something less gloomy. I told her that a lot of kids have problems with their feelings and that many hurt themselves, and that I wanted to tell other kids and parents about that by writing their stories. The irony is that she never asked why I was writing about Gabriella. Before she could ask, I told her I was writing about matters other than suicide as well.

But I don't think Gabriella told her exactly what I was doing, in terms of the suicide book, and I sensed that, so I didn't say anything more about it, either. Gabriella had winked at me as a signal not to say anything beyond the explanation that she was taking me to the Goth club because I was writing about teenage life and culture. So I was viewed as sort of Gabriella's date. I believe, too, that Gabriella's mother was so used to Gabriella doing whatever she pleased that it was not uncommon to have people over to the house, and so this was pretty normal. Gabriella was grown now, or growing up, and her mother did not respect Gabriella's father or the men in the house, and they (the women) ruled the roost, as it were.

Gabriella's mom told me, "As a parent, I feel all kids should have appropriate sexual relations." I asked what she meant, she explained:

> When I say "appropriate" sex [fingers indicating quotation marks], I mean I don't want my kids involved in anything forced. I also don't want my girls having unnatural sex, like lesbian orgies and that kinda thing. I consider that to be wrong, because it goes against nature. I don't wanna read about my girls having sex in weird places. And, above all, I don't want my kids having sex with relatives, strangers, or other ethnics.

I was curious what she meant by "other ethnics" but didn't dare to ask.

I had intended to discuss Gabriella with her mother, but when I got there, Gabriella pulled me aside and said, "Let's just see what she thinks about life."

Gabriella perceived all her relationships, whether with girls or with boys, as hurtful, because she saw those situations as flawed from the start. Her confusion about her own sexuality intensified when she had a relationship with a girl. The girl cared little for her and slept around—just as Gabriella's father had done to her mother. Her relationships were being played out just as she had witnessed relationships transpiring during her early childhood, because we always mirror our family life, until we get old enough and smart enough to stop doing it. If a kid is rejected at home, she may mimic that behavior so that she's rejected everywhere, in all the most crucial relationships—just as her parents rejected her.

Gabriella's method of coping with her "problem" is wrapped up in diary entries with subtle hidden meanings. Her note is as dramatic and revealing as others I've seen. Her situation happens to be about "love," but it could be about anything—parents, weight loss, incest, loneliness. Nonetheless, as a suicidal person, she is unwilling to accept the disturbance and states plainly that the pain is too much for her to bear.

And so, to a certain extent, Gabriella's suicide notes/diaries, like all the others, represent a "suicide problem" that has to be unraveled and decoded: What happened? When? Where? With whom? It is emotional detective work. None of these narratives should be seen simply as individual notes. They are three-dimensional social and emotional testimonies that travel well beyond the individual person who is experiencing deep pain (and, in two cases here, actually committed suicide). In this case, I had a chance to talk with Gabriella's mother. Even so, I could discern only fragments about Gabriella's ethnic background, which, coupled with place, might have told me more about the religious and cultural ideas that informed the social roles within her home and society.

In her note, Gabriella is angry, sarcastic, and harried. She calls her letters "death messages," and they reveal the pains of several disturbed relationships. These very personal statements reek of trauma. She's confused about her sexuality, makes claims to be a lesbian at thirteen, and then falls in love with a boy at sixteen (which she has vowed all her young life never to do). He raped her on their first date and, to make matters much worse, got her pregnant.

Her lesbianism is not, perhaps, entirely genuine, but rather, at some level, an escape from the male presence.

Dear Diary,

So I haven't been telling all. I knew this would come out at some time or another, but I wasn't sure when: I have broken the carnal lesbian rule. I have betrayed my sisters and eroticized my own oppression. I never thought it would happen to me—never thought I could stray so far from what I've always known; that I am a lesbian; that I love women. But for the first time in my entire life, I have been sleeping with a boy.

Gabriella notes that life is painful, and that she wants immediate release from the pain, but she wants sex from the boy she now hates:

The thing is, I think if we had sex, I'd be OK. I'd be able to think a little more clearly, and it's so much more than that now. I'd be settling.

It is no secret that kids who report suicidal events associate them most often with severe family problems and disturbed family relationships. In that way, Gabriella is a more textbook case than the other kids. A week after the conversation with Gabriella's mother, Gabriella and I met again, to continue our conversation and talk about her suicide attempts. It was a cool evening, with a light drizzle falling in the city. Gabriella walked in looking like she was going clubbing. Her hair was pulled back in a ponytail and her nails were bright red to match her lipstick, all draped together with hip-hugging jeans, suede blouse, and high-heeled shoes.

She ordered tea and immediately began to discuss her life in an almost tattletale fashion. I asked why she could talk about her suicide attempts with such a carefree attitude.

First of all, I'm out of that now, and I know I don't have to ever deal with him again if I choose not to. I felt like a waste as a lesbian. I felt there was absolutely nothing no one could do for me. I was a waste.

Apparently, she had misunderstood me and thought I had asked about her "sweetheart." When I corrected her, she said the entries in the diary I read were part of three full diaries about this boy who she once loved but now hated. She wanted to talk about the suicide attempts, and though her giddiness made me feel uneasy, I sat and listened.

I have to admit, it wasn't something that was strongly thought out, this jumping off his building. I can tell you now that the reason I wanted to do it was because I wanted him to feel the full impact of my act. It was not planned so much as spontaneous, because we used to go to the top of his building and smoke so the opportunities were there. But I also had feelings about the trains, too. I wanted it to be quick, not something that would take too long. I wanted it to be in his hands.

This last statement hints at something akin to emotional revenge, so I asked her how close she came to actually committing suicide. I wanted to see how much of her act was thought and how much was action. She looked at me with a slightly serious frown.

Well, my thoughts were definitely there, and I did go to the edge of the building, and did stand at the rim of the subway tracks and kinda watched and thought about what would happen. And in my mind I've been there a number of times. I thought about the screech of the train and lights glaring down the tracks and what it must feel like to have those lights hit me when I jumped. And his standing there watching, to witness it all, and making him suffer for what he'd done to me.

So, emotionally I've definitely been there, but physically I could only get so close, because as much as I want all of these things to end, I also had a strong fear of death. But, at the same time, it's a fear I overcome every time I think about how humiliated I was by him. I also know how easy it is to go back to those feeling of killing myself, because all these feelings I have for him have not totally subsided.

Gabriella tried to clarify some of the contradictory issues. For example, she says she hates men, yet she found herself thinking not just about suicide but about suicide over a boy. I asked her to explain.

The only reason why this got that way was that he was such a different-looking, different-acting, unusual kinda boy. He wasn't the macho type. He was like no other male person I had ever met or knew. But, in a strange sense, he was not like a man to me, either. I know that sounds bizarre, because the things I was really attracted to about him were really, really male.

One question I had for the kids like Gabriella was about what stopped them from committing suicide. I thought her answer might provide a way to help other kids in similar circumstances.

I guess the answer to that question is I just stopped myself from going forward with it. I got the feeling that I shouldn't do it without it having the maximum impact. What would the maximum impact be? Well, that would happen only if he were there with me when I died. I don't think it would have made the maximum impact otherwise.

I reminded Gabriella again that she was still focused on the boy, and that even her last wish was about a male. She explained:

Well, that's true if you only consider one part of the thing. The other part is I would have wanted the whole thing to be blood on his hands. The full impact would have been only when he would be standing beside me.

I wanted him to be guilty, too, you see, because I had been carrying around so much guilt about this whole pregnancy thing, and he did the exact same thing I did, yet he's able to live with that and I'm not.

My questions made Gabriella think about what her own suicide would mean.

In a sense, it would mean that I would be punishing myself. I've always said that men are the absolute downfall of any woman, and it would kinda bear testimony to that, in my mind. But, at the same time, I'm in the same boat as all these other women who have killed themselves over men, and I certainly don't want to be part of that.

Kids write suicide notes for many reasons, but the most consistent reason I heard was that they had little control over their own lives. They write suicide notes so they can have the last word, a little bit of power, or, in the case of Gabriella, a little of both.

I wrote this note because I wanted to be clear. Everybody gets their last word in, their last hint of anger, remorse out, things that they want to say to whomever. I wanted to be totally clear that whoever was gonna find that note knew why I had done what I'd done. I didn't want someone else to put those words in my mouth, and I didn't want anyone to speculate about why I had done it. But, at the same time, I was sorta embarrassed about it. And the embarrassment was part of the reason why.

I have always written letters, kept a diary, had a travel journal. And he would read my journals on and off. I would allow him to read about some of my feelings, and the more I got to know him, the more I wanted him to know how I felt about him.

Look, I didn't say a lot of explicit things in my suicide note about being pregnant, or that I didn't want the baby, and that I wanted him to suffer and all of that, because I was a little bit worried that he would find my journal and read it. And, at the same time, I was constantly changing, and I would go on and off and on and off. You see, a lot of the time, when I was mad, I would deal with my feeling in a different way.

But, at the same time, there never was a time when things were perfect. There was never a time when things were totally bad, either. It was always a mix of the two. I was convinced that our relationship had to end in some dramatic way. It couldn't just die out, because it was always so volatile.

So something was bound to happen. I didn't know what to do. I wasn't talking to anybody. I wasn't writing about it. I was kinda living in my own little world, and that world was wrapped up in a lot of fear. I still feel ambivalent about it.

Even though I wasn't talking to anybody, I still had close friends, where we would read each other's journals and spend time together. It was too much, because I couldn't even tell my friends about him and the situation I was in.

Gabriella's network of shared feelings is expressed here, and how she kept hurting herself.

I was embarrassed because, after all of my man-hating, and all of my hypocrisy, that I would not only would be a hypocrite in words but in actions. But the killing part was the idea of craving something you hate. There is nothing more humiliating than to crave something you hate. And to let other people know about that is even worse. Internally, I was punishing myself.

In her diary, she noted:

I was thinking while I was laying there all I wanted was nothing but my girlfriends—my pussy loving girlfriends—I wanted them to bust into my room, remind me of who I was, where I should be, who I should be fucking. I wanted them to rush in and carry me off in a lesbian blaze of glory, I wanted them to lap me up and hold me afterwards, and I wanted to never see his stupid face again.

The idea of loving someone (indeed, something) that you hate is both powerful and quite intriguing. Gabriella was desperately trying to engage in a kind of sexual exorcism—to rid herself of the hatred that she had for father (the symbol for all men) against the backdrop of making the claim that she is a lesbian. She never really indicates that she is bisexual. Her suicide narratives and rite can also be regarded as a way to inflict pain on her father and, by proxy, her boyfriend. She wants them to assume control of her pain, to claim it and make it their lifelong possession, in much the way she had to contend with this pain throughout her adolescent life. The last I heard, she did not have the baby.

Dear Diary

I am hurt, but I claim responsibility for it. I should have known better. I did know better, but I decided to go against my best judgment. I am over you. I can't stand the ambivalence—like you one today, hate you the next. Why did I trust you? Because I wanted to. Now I feel stupid and I feel used . . . I'm tired of pulling myself up.

Gabriella told me:

Now this is really ironic. I was volunteering at an abortion clinic, where I was out as a lesbian, so I couldn't go there and tell them I was pregnant. I couldn't go there at all with this mess. All this was running around in my head.

Now, that was the first time I felt all alone, because there was no one I could talk to. There was no place I could go. And there was no way I could have a baby now. I can't do that. I was so embarrassed, and I'm thinking all of this. I knew right then and there this had to end in a bang.

Things were getting outta control. I wasn't sleeping. He wasn't answering his phone, and I felt desperate. I took the train to his place, and as I stood on the tracks I walked closer and closer to the yellow line and put my foot right on the edge, with it sticking out over the platform. I could hear the train getting closer. But I pulled back, because I wanted him to be there and he wasn't. He was probably on his roof.

Well, I knew he went to the roof, which was where he always goes, and I figured he must be up there. So I went up there, too. I thought, *I'll go up and jump off the building right in front of him*, and that would be it. I thought about his being there and what impact that would have on his head forever and ever.

My death would be on his hands, witnessed by him. I felt power when I thought about killing myself, when I thought about jumping off that building and jumping in front of that train . . . But that one moment, when I stood there ready to jump, this was the one thing that was mine. He couldn't talk me out of it. It was a one-night-only thing, a one-time-only, couldn't-do-it-again type thing.

It was something that belonged to me, and that was empowering. It had everything to do with him, but at the same time, it had nothing to do with him. I felt like he didn't have the power to kill me but I had the power to kill myself.

AFTERWORD

I sing sometimes for the war that I fight,
'cause every tool is a weapon, if you hold it right.
—*Ani DiFranco, "My IQ"*

American kids are losing ground, showing all the symptoms of
social, parental, and personal neglect. Many are left to fend for
themselves, and barely manage. Teenage suicides continue and
grown-ups do not seem to be getting the point. Our collective
failure to confront the rate at which our teens are self-destruct-
ing is one of the reasons I have written this book. Although
school shootings have opened the nation's eyes to youth violence
and have inspired a full-scale examination, teen suicide is still
shrouded in denial, though it would be difficult to find an adult
in America who does not know at least one seriously troubled or
disturbed teenager—either within their own family or among the
families of friends or relatives. And most would probably admit
that they have no idea how to understand a problem that threatens to tear the American family apart.

Family life and structure is a key aspect of this book, and these
notes about the various experiences of these kids explode the
myth of two-parent families and expose a raw nerve, as it were,
of parent and teen socialization. Heretofore, the mantra has
been that a child's success is largely determined by a two-parent

household. But a recurring theme in all of the teen suicide notes is a breakdown in the family structure. And it is also clear that this is an intergenerational issue.

The annual suicide rate among American teenagers ages fifteen to nineteen has more than tripled since the 1950s, from fewer than 2.7 suicides to more than 8.71 suicides per 100,000 people in 2014. It is worth noting that, within this teenage group, the suicide rate increased dramatically with age. For example, in 2014 the suicide rate among fifteen-year-old males was 7.47 per 100,000 people, while among nineteen-year-old males the rate was 17.47 per 100,000 people. The Centers for Disease Control reported that, from 2000 to 2014, there were 24,679 deaths among teenagers ages fifteen to nineteen, and the annual number of deaths from suicide has been increasing for the past ten years.[1]

Among young people fifteen to twenty-four years old, suicide is currently the second leading cause of death, exceeded only by unintentional injury. More teenagers and young adults die from suicide than from cancer, heart disease, AIDS, birth defects, stroke, pneumonia, influenza, and chronic lung disease combined. Among ten- to twenty-four-year-olds in the United States, overall age-adjusted suicide rates by sex fluctuated somewhat during 1994 to 2012, but rates among males were consistently much higher than among females. In 1994, rates were 15.7 suicides per 100,000 males, compared with 2.7 suicides per 100,000 females. In 2012, rates were 11.9 suicides among 100,000 males, compared with 3.2 suicides among 100,000 females—male suicides had gone down significantly, but female suicide increased slightly.[2]

According to the Centers for Disease Control, the 2011 Youth Risk Behavior survey found that almost 16 percent of students in grades nine to twelve had seriously thought about suicide, and 7.8 percent (1 in 13 students) had attempted suicide one or more times during the past year. The survey also found that suicide-related thoughts are common among high school students: more than 1 in 7 students nationwide seriously considered attempting suicide in the twelve months prior to the survey. Suicides among kids ages ten to fourteen increased by 260.74 percent from 1981 to 2014.[3]

Whether they were from wealthy homes, from solid middle-class families, or from poor households, the anguish of the teens I talked with is deeply felt, across the board. These young people hold up an enlarged mirror to the frustrations, anger, and spiritual loss so pervasive in many teens' lives today. This work also indicates that the thought of committing suicide and the writing of suicidal notes are common among teenagers.

Remarkably few books have been written about teens who write suicide notes, and none has examined the suicide writings of these troubled young people in depth. Jack Gibbs's *Suicide* covers the history of suicide and offers some rather fascinating examples of suicide through the ages.[4] Teenagers are not specific to Gibbs's argument, however.

The implicit demographic context of the suicide notes and interviews profiled here (including race and gender, class and family income, rural or suburban environment, educational achievement, one- or two-parent households, and time frame) provides a nuanced sense of teenage suicide. The notes are also a deep meditation, if you will, on family life as a "nuclear society." Children and teenagers are deeply shaped by—and in some cases destroyed by—the nuclear society that we call family life. Conventional wisdom has indicated that a two-parent household is ideal, but the narratives in this text discredit that idea and expose sordid, abusive, and destructive parental practices that have been deployed to impose cruelty on children and teenagers.

The much larger question is how these narratives, which took place during the 1990s and early 2000, can be seen and understood today. The narratives are powerful—raw, brutal, insightful, and painful—but the real gist of the narratives is that certain variables maintain themselves and, of course, are affected by technology. The notion of writing journals, diaries, and letters as a form of technology, and how this will transmogrify among a generation of youths who have been digitally connected since childhood—and certainly in the wake of the advent of social media, where all sorts of notes and ideas are written by teenagers—is anyone's guess. In such a context, ethnography as immersive work becomes much more expansive, and, frankly, if a researcher today does not know where to look, many parasuicidal notes will never be found. These days, a lot of teenagers (and grown people) film all sorts of things on their cell phones, from sexual encounters to police killings of unarmed citizens, and who is to say a suicide will not be filmed? One such attempt was made by seventeen-year-old Nala Morrison and was highlighted on YouTube in 2014, and Tucker (chapter 5) told me of filming a suicide note.

It also is important to note the creative aspect of these parasuicidal notes and to understand that the suicide note may not, in fact, be an artifact to explain an actual suicide. Only two of the kids profiled here committed suicide, and their narratives, so to speak, are refracted through the testimony of friends and family. This needs to be emphasized: many of the journals and letters detail cathartic emotional highs and lows, but most of these kids survived. The question is how and under what circumstances.

We are facing a new generation of kids who are vastly different in mind and soul from those who came before. To some millennials, life seems so meaningless that they are willing to die—not for country, religion, or even family but as a clear sign of their refusal to cooperate with a society they consider so critically unjust that they want to escape from it permanently.

It's not clear, however, that the issue rests solely on American society. These narratives clearly indicate that the American family as a unit of socialization, broken down further by ethnicity, class, social mores, and religious beliefs, is at the core of many teen suicides. Perhaps, therefore, it is critically important to examine mental health within the context of parenting and unresolved intergenerational trauma. This, it seems to me, cannot be emphasized enough. The refusal to cooperate is a damning thing in our society, because we are obsessed with forcing our kids to do just that. Parents are a symbolic stand-in for society, and kids are engaging in a culture of refusal because there is angst about society writ large. My textual reading is that teenagers are clearly angry with, if not mortified by their parents, who are representative of the larger adult world order.

In many ways, kids ask the same questions they have always asked. They are trying to figure out what's going on in their lives. Their bodies confuse them, and they are anxious about which of their many feelings should prevail. They are aware of an underlying conflict and are asking questions about who they are, and that puzzles them, because they feel different, and so they act out what they are feeling. They are asking questions about what is expected of them and about their society, which refuses to accept them because they are different. This sense of being different is the fundamental basis of their suicidal feelings and actions. The task of growing up and coming to terms with their bodies and emotions against the backdrop of parental and societal expectations is a kind of adolescent clash with the adult world. These young people are trying to figure out how they fit into a family structure they find inhibiting.

And, in this sense, several of these narratives make it clear that, somewhere in society, there is a place where they can fit in, whether in subcultures of society, such as the East Village, or elsewhere, such as going on the road. Here, they can feel free enough to be liberated from debasement or emotional pain exacted by parents. I believe this is the real key. Kids are leaving their homes and reinventing themselves, and this is as it should be, but they are not only doing it because of beatings, sexual abuse, or parental neglect. The pain of adolescence, family conflicts, and struggles with friends and teachers—all the discomforts and confusions in our kids' heads—makes them challenge life itself, to the point where far too many have become obsessed with suicide as a way to end it all.

Understanding teen suicide requires respect for teens' insights and an understanding of history and culture, from many different points of view. I believe this to be a critical point. For decades, we have wondered whether there is a crucial moment that bridges the transition between childhood and adulthood, and what special rite, if any, marks this passage. Is there any specific event, for example, that signifies that change? The senior prom or debutante ball? The first sexual encounter? Violence or drug use? Joining the army? Or the first job that carries adult responsibility? This idea of a rite of passage is important, but it seems to me that the narratives raise a much larger question about the way adults see themselves and thus reinvent themselves in the form of their children, transmitting humanity and the overriding culture or purpose that undergirds it.

At issue, then, is the intergenerational way of living in and imagining a particular family life and structure within the context of a much larger society. What, for instance, does it mean to be an "American" child in a country of immigrants who bring with them various ways of imagining man, woman, child, son, and daughter? These are and have been documented as cruel and complex cauldrons of familial socialization and childhood angst. The rite of passage, as such, is the socialization of the individual in society through the familial eye of the needle. The notes we've looked at here ask, What should family structure and life look like? What are its ideals, mores, and mechanisms for the adolescent? How does adult life procreate as a social being? The real and apparent tension in these notes relates to the psychodynamics of family life.

From a sociological perspective, it seems to me that poor people, especially visible minority folks, have been derided for the collapse of their family structure, yet the narratives here clearly indicate that all is not well in the two-parent, 1950s-style conceptualizations of family life, either. Lack of love and unhealthy modes of parental discipline are huge aspects of the narratives. One even wonders whether two-parent households are necessary. Wouldn't it perhaps be better to have just one responsible and loving parent? Finally, what does being a responsible parent mean, since all human beings have psychological and emotional baggage?

Most Americans do not believe that American society includes any rites of passage at all. But America has one of the highest teen suicide rates in the world, in addition to an unrecorded and therefore unknown number of additional attempts, and American teens are—at one and the same time—both escaping death and succeeding in killing themselves at unprecedented rates. Indeed, you could argue that, in twenty-first-century America, suicide and suicide attempts are the real rites of passage for teenagers, that this ritual of intentional harm and self-induced risk taking —such as through drug misuse, hanging, shooting, anorexia, or wrist slitting—characterizes the transition that thrusts our kids into adulthood.

Of course, the kids who wrote these notes represent too small a sample to make such broad assertions, but our teens are indulging in rituals that are different but similar to older societies in which boys and girls undergo risks in order to become men or women. In northwestern Zambia, for example, anthropologist Victor Turner documented such a ritual initiation:

> Although both boys and girls undergo initiation ceremonies, the form and purpose of the ceremonies differ widely in either case. Boys, for instance, are circumcised, but there is no cliterodectomy of girls. Boys are initiated collectively, girls individually. Boys are initiated before and girls at the onset of puberty. The main purpose of boys' initiation is to inculcate tribal values, hunting skill, and sexual instruction; that of girls' initiation is to prepare them for marriage, which follows immediately in the great majority of cases. Boys are secluded and taught in the bush; a grass hut is built in the village itself for girls.[5]

There are inherent dangers in these seemingly normal rituals, and thus the idea of the death risk as a youthful act is not strange. It is actually as old as time. What is happening to the American teen is really not very different, except for one important fact: too many kids are succeeding in killing themselves. But the notes are not so much about these rituals as they are about the more simple, salient point of growing up.

The transition from child to adult in American life is quite complex, and looking closely, we can see the focus in the narratives as this: looking at the family unit as a long-term emotional and psychological incubator for people who eventually become adults.

What are the rites, passed along from one generation to another, that confer on adults the ability to become a healthy parent? A child does not come with a manual. Social norms become the manual. So, what are these? How does a parent learn to be a parent? Is this a ritual of some kind and, if so, what is it? How is it transmitted? What role does gender play in the creation of a parent? These are really the larger questions that I try to bring into the narratives.

American teenagers, unlike the children who experience structured and monitored rituals in the Ndembu and other societies, have no village elders who safeguard the passage with age-old and well-established guidelines. There are no rules of engagement. The ritual, as such, of growing up and passing from childhood to adulthood is a refrain here. How does this work in industrialized countries? Is there a difference between, say, a rural area and a metropolitan area? This requires more comparative elaboration than space allows, but we can assume that kids simply improvise—inventing as they go along. They copy friends; latch on to things they see on television, the Internet or in movies; or mimic the behavior and lyrics of their favorite music gurus. I should note that the teenagers I worked with indicated that suicidal note writing was common among teenagers. And many teenagers have also adopted or developed different ways to announce that they intend to kill themselves.

Thus, these teen narratives have an internal logic all their own, and that logic should or must be amplified if we are to understand teenage suicide within the context of the family. Diagramming these narratives can reveal certain recurring fact patterns. These fact patterns, in turn, indicate that these teenagers are reacting to horrific circumstances within a family structure: humiliation, beatings, sexual abuse, or psychological degradation. The notes are sometimes shocking and sometimes enlightening, as most of the teenagers (those who did not actually kill themselves) used suicide narratives as a means of emotional catharsis, to seek attention, or to call attention to their suffering within the "ideal" framework of family life.

One night, outside a well-known Goth hangout in Greenwich Village, I talked to a kid wearing high, laced-up black boots, a nose ring connected to an earring by a silver chain, and a white skull-and-bones neckpiece hanging down over a black leather vest. In a barely audible voice, he said:

> We all gotta die sometime. Death can be beautiful. I'd rather die now than wait till I'm old as my parents, wrinkled and sexless, holding onto the keys of a new Mercedes, living happily ever miserably after in a dying culture.

Though we might not find it easy to understand our teens' culture of refusal, we urgently need to recognize that we live in a changed world and that their generation is involved in defining a pivotal collective moment. So far, however, the truth and importance of this appears to be lost on most adults. The solution is not as easy to identify as the problem, but answers can be found if we just open our eyes to the problem. Look at society. Look at our kids. Look at ourselves. Kids are difficult, complex beings, no doubt, but kids committing suicide think no one understands. And they are right. Most parents don't understand.

Though my own teenage son has not shown suicidal tendencies, I am often at wits' end to understand him, and I frequently have sought professional guidance to help me decide how to cope with his not always understandable behavior. Coping with suicidal behavior, however, on top of everything else, must be especially daunting.

The teenage years are tough on everybody. And there is no simple, magical solution that applies to everyone. The solutions, like the causes, are multiple, layered, and confound. But we have to address them, and we have to continue learning ways to help our kids create more positive behaviors. As one parent said to me:

> What else can we do? If we do nothing, they [our kids] become nothing. If we do too much, they rebel. If we sit back, we are lousy parents. We are trapped, aren't we?

In some ways, this is adolescent assertion of the self as kids struggle with their sexuality, listen to music their parents do not like, or sport haircuts and clothing that might be a bit off-putting to parents. But parents are only trapped in their own illusions if they don't listen, don't observe, and don't care, and a lot of parents don't know how to help their kids. Megan (chapter 3) said as much to me after I talked with her mother: "They [parents] also have problems of their own, issues and feelings they don't deal with, and these always get transferred to their children, who act as mirrors for them, just as parents do for the kids."

Megan's statement is the essence of the notes, the pure tension of the text in a nuts-and-bolts sense. It describes perfectly the larger conundrum of family life in America: the unresolved intergenerational transfer of trauma, pain, sexual anxiety, and inability to love. Tolstoy, in *Anna Karenina*, likens the inability to love to hell itself.

Teen suicide, like a lot of teen behavior, is complicated and involves the interplay of many different elements. America began to form its modern makeup in the 1950s, developing a singularly materialistic identity and creating a middle class large enough to sustain a consumer-oriented economy that has brought unprecedented wealth to its capitalist institutions, and in this, the seeds were sown for our current malaise. Today, our twenty-one million teenagers spend more than $155 billion a year and influence their parents to spend another $150 billion.[6] In his book *An All-Consuming Century*, writer Gary Cross argues, "This society of goods is not merely the inevitable consequence of mass production or the manipulation of merchandisers. It is a choice, never consciously made, to define self and community through the ownership of goods."[7]

This trend to define ourselves in terms of what we own has prompted marketers to adopt an anthropological approach to studying teen culture and analyzing their behaviors. But not enough has been done to understand teenagers themselves, and it is ironic and tragic that this same period of unprecedented affluence has corresponded with such high rates of suicide among teenagers. In fact, this correlation is so disturbing that parents should see in it a warning that there is more to life than shopping. The increased availability of information has created kids who are much more open-minded than previous generations, simply because there isn't much they haven't seen. Maturity is expected much sooner from us than was expected in generations before us. Parents need to learn how to evolve, listen, and look for the signs in their kids, and in themselves.

Kids often go even further within themselves and look for quick fixes on the outside. They go to the Internet, to music, to the malls, and hot new clubs, all as a way to express how they feel. Megan told me:

We are at the crossroads here in America, where parents have to listen to kids and kids have to listen to adults, maybe for the first time. I think parents have to understand that we are dealing with a world that's a lot different than twenty years ago. What drives kids into alternative lifestyles, experimentation, and rock music—Goth-loving freak behavior—is a need to get a message across that difference has to be accepted. The reasons are varied, but it's really about a feeling of being different, feeling different, and thinking differently.

The point—or perhaps the problem—is that there is adolescent culture and then there is adult culture. Parents may like Stravinsky and not understand their kids' attraction to the dark music of Marilyn Manson, to rap music (which is white suburban kids' current choice), or—at one time—to the Beatles. I overheard one white corporate commuter say he hates the sound of rap music, and I assume this is exactly what his father said about him listening to rock and roll, back in the day. These cultures clash, but they need not do so, because it is precisely new technologies like the Internet that may help to overcome the clash.

Gita told me:

> Parents, and adults in general, don't understand their kids' world, or they don't understand their kids and therefore don't understand the kids' place in the world. Of all the kids I've met and hung out with, one thing is certain: most of them feel "different."

This "difference" is really about all forms and kinds of difference: race, age, gender. It is about acceptance and inclusion. It is about an honest conversation America should be having with itself, all the time, as a kind of ongoing collective talking cure.

Another major difference this generation faces is related to the information age. The Internet exposes kids to enormous amounts of raw and highly complex information, at much younger ages, than in previous generations. But technology is not to blame; it's just making something everyone would have done before much easier to get at. In some ways, parents even depend on their kids to deal with much of the new technology, and as a result, they often relinquish control of its use. As one high school teen from Brooklyn said, "My parents can barely work their VCRs, so they always have to ask me to fix their computer. How are they gonna keep me from logging on to porn sites?"

The "differentness" that Gita, Megan, and others talk about comes from kids' lack of a sense of belonging, and this, along with a fascination with change, will often lead them to find attractive what their parents find repulsive: tattoos, death, or self-mutilation. As Gita told me, "I belong to this generation referred to as 'apathetic youth,' though kids more than ever seem aware of the problems facing the world, and concerned with finding solutions."

The kids in this book discussed the issues of death, apathy, and refusal. And although some shared horror stories of incest, loveless relationships, mindless competitiveness, and the suburbs from hell, others pointed to the culture we live in: the dead-end malls, the boredom, the purposelessness of life, and especially, the cultural hypocrisy. That hypocrisy is most evident in the huge profits to be made from exploiting and fetishizing the teenage body—a reality not lost on our teens, who are aware of how teenage consumption patterns are a key aspect of the American economy.

But malls, the Internet, and hot new stuff have no soul. It's dead inside, just like a fast-food burger at McDonald's. I was visiting Toronto several years ago, at the same time that a well-known rinpoche, or Tibetan Buddhist monk, was visiting the city. The local chamber of commerce decided to offer the rinpoche a tour of an indoor mall that ran along four city blocks. At the time, this mall was one of the largest in the world.

When the rinpoche finally emerged from the tour, his eyes were filled with tears. When his hosts asked him what in the mall had moved him to such a reaction, he paused thoughtfully and answered sadly, "It's so much of what's not enough."

Sociologist Donna Gaines eloquently stated in her book *Teenage Wasteland*, "In the social order of the American high school, teens are expected to do what they are told—make the grade, win the prize, play the game. Kids who refuse have always found something else to do. Sometimes it kills them; sometimes it sets them free."[8]

The dead-end nature of the culture is mirrored in our kids' eyes, in their clothes, in the music they listen to, and in everything else. These are the ones who are affected the most by their dysfunctional homes, abuse, or their sexuality. Many feel that they are an invisible minority, and the number of teenagers who try to kill themselves increases every decade.

Gender plays a key role in suicide styles. Girls attempt suicide by cutting their wrists or overdosing on drugs, whereas boys tend to use more physically violent means such as hanging, guns, car crashes, or jumps from buildings. Two studies have reported the following sex differences: "Females appear to be less direct and less negative in their communications about the forthcoming suicide; females exhibit greater concern for others whom they know interpersonally; females express greater negative emotions, specifically, despondency, grief, and disappointment; and females appear to be more disorganized in their writings."[9]

Although Gita's writing was especially compelling and the most organized of all the teens profiled, the question is in what ways do the narratives reflect this assessment?

Candy's note (chapter 3), for instance, was addressed to a friend: "If you leave while my heart is wide open you will be leaving me to bleed to death." The note indicates trauma, and it reveals the same desperation we see with others who attempt suicide. Although it is brief, the note does not, on first viewing, seem to indicate her suicide, and in that way, it is not atypical. Many suicide notes do not use the word *suicide* in them or mention dying. However, it does show that every suicide note is different and that one cannot tell what a person who is about to commit suicide is thinking. The reason Candy wrote a note becomes clearer as we scan through it, because we start to see that her reason is to leave a last testament, a dying declaration, a last word, uninterrupted, unchallenged—a last record that says, "I exist."

Tucker, a gay kid who attempted suicide, typically asks the same kinds of questions of himself as other kids ask: Who am I? Where do I fit? How can I get out the anxiety I feel? Am I gay? Will I be a man? Will I get married? Am I pretty enough? How can I survive these teenage years? How can I get people to respect my religion? These are the issues confronting teenagers everywhere. And if all teenagers go through similar experiences, then the actions of a kid like Tucker are really a microcosm of what most teens in this country feel, regardless of income, ethnicity, or family location. These are the questions of this generation.

I think Tucker's struggle with being gay is an excellent example of the interpretive analysis hugging the road of the narratives. These narratives mirror teens' larger issues, especially issues of sexual orientation. The deeper point is that being a child is not a fixed enterprise from generation to generation. This makes parenting more a game of trying to arrange moving adolescent pieces than anything else. For example, the discussion about the Internet has changed dramatically since the 1990s, the period covered in these narratives. Today, a lot of children have cell phones. How has this changed courting and hanging out with

boys or girls? What about porn? There is video chatting. There
is no hiding and sneaking anymore; just log on. Sexting? This is
a brave new world for children and teenagers. How do parents
adjust to technological changes that affect the raising of children
who can easily explore the taboo world of adults?

Our kids don't know who to trust, keep everything inside
themselves, and feel like the weight of the world is on their
shoulders. These kids explode, as was seen in the tragedy at Sandy
Hook Elementary. Enoch (chapter 2) told me:

> You remember when they started the label of the "trench coat ma-
> fia" as a way to define all kids—they started to paint all kids in
> trench coats as murderers and potential murderers. Well, it's this
> kind of thing that gets us kids pissed off, because it lumps all of
> us together, and we refuse to cooperate with adults even more, by
> joining obscure cults, gangs, and stuff.

As part of philanthropist George Soros's Open Society Institute
Project on Death in America, I convened a group of teenagers,
ages thirteen to seventeen, to talk about death at an early age.
One fourteen-year-old with his cap pulled to the side of his head
casually raised his hand and said, matter-of-factly, "When I go
out every day, I think more about killing than I do about dying."
It was a piercing moment, and the other kids looked on, nodding
silently, because they held similar views. Although some teens
think about killing themselves, they often think about killing
others as well. Those others can be family members, other kids, or
strangers who have harassed them, disrespected them, or treated
them with disdain.

Suicide and homicide are on the same path; one indicates
contempt for the self and the other shows contempt for others.

The difference between a kid who kills and one who commits suicide is stark, because the killer of others shows little feeling or empathy—and even extreme hatred—for parents, teachers, or society, more generally, and doesn't feel in the least that he or she needs help. The self-killer feels the same way, but turns the anger inward.

Kids going through psychological, emotional, and physical changes often are moved to act in ways that are aggressive for no apparent reason. A slight brush by another person, a look or a glance in their direction, rejection by a girl, any number of seemingly meaningless gestures can cause a kid to react violently. And such violent reaction, according to more recent data, is more of a problem among boys than girls, because boys, not girls, kill. Older boys (ages fifteen to nineteen) kill at a rate seven times that of boys under fifteen.

They have figured out the world hates them, and they respond by hating back, as would most people. They are exacting revenge on a world that has hurt them. The kid who kills himself is just as angry at parents, teachers, and others, but instead of forcing that anger on others, he exacts revenge on himself, through suicide, to make others suffer by their loss. They are willing to sacrifice themselves, punishing others by punishing themselves. Thus, the kid who kills others and the kid who kills herself have one thing in common: a lack of caring from the world.

There are times when kids live in a world few adults can understand. Although this age-defined period is called teenagehood, what we are really facing, according to some, is the failure to see kids as "beginner adults." Such critics argue that we pamper our kids into believing that the years from thirteen to nineteen have been given to them as a kind of "time-out gift," during which they are not responsible to anything or anybody but themselves and are free to experiment with life, to act up, hang low, drop out, or do whatever they wish.

Thomas Hine, for instance, contends that "teenager" is a social construct that has outlived its usefulness. According to Hine, if we stopped treating kids as "teenagers" and started treating them as "beginner adults"—giving them jobs and responsibility and expecting them to perform like young adults—we would not have the delinquency, rebelliousness, identity issues, crime, or perhaps even the high-risk personal behavior, such as suicide, that is associated with this group.[10]

But failure to treat our kids as young adults isn't even half the problem. The real problem is the failure to treat them like real people, and perhaps we should think about how we can deconstruct or at least change adult life. More often than not, parents don't see that kids are scared, vulnerable, and looking to them for the love, support, and direction they will need, now and forever, to survive. As soon as kids start to talk, many parents assume their job is done. But the job of a parent is never done, which is why so many parents should take responsibility for the kids they so often disregard. Because "those" clothes, "that" music, and kids' every action is a direct result of their upbringing.

If a child happens to be gay or lesbian and a parent keeps telling them they're abnormal and strange because of that, it's going to affect those kids. If a child is weak or vulnerable and is called "faggot," he or she won't understand how to process that. They are too young. If children are beaten, abused, assaulted, or verbally disregarded, all of these things will affect them, push them deeper into their shells, and make them act out in a way that will reflect their treatment.

Kids try to fix their own problems by indulging in a number of ritual acts that they feel will help them cope with pain, anger, rage, and other strong emotions they believe might get out of control. These "fixes" include using a host of popular drugs, including but not limited to marijuana, ecstasy, cocaine, alcohol, or LSD. More "useful" fixes might include talking-out sessions, writing in diaries or journals, meditation in places of peace, exercising, having sex, masturbating, or self-mutilation. Other possible solutions might include seeking clinical help, maintaining friends one's parents don't like but the kids do, talking to respected adults, and self-healing and learning in nontraditional settings.

Gabriella (chapter 10) told me:

> I'd seek therapy. Especially If I knew someone who was going through what I was going through. I think therapy on a regular basis would make a difference.

Gita (chapter 6) seems to agree:

> I think you gotta get all that stuff outta your head. Since girls in particular have so much emotion and are more willing than boys to talk about stuff, maybe having someone to talk to all the time would be a good idea. That could be counselors they could call—twenty-four hours a day would be good.

Keeping a journal and using writing as cure is one way to assuage anxiety. By doing so, young people use writing in a therapeutic way, exposing themselves to the rawness of their experiences, revealing a certain truth about themselves, family, and friends. For example, Boots's journal (chapter 7) provides a window for us, the reader, to understand him and to witness his deepest, darkest secrets. In one passage, he revealed:

I didn't want to be like my parents, and I saw my life following the same path as theirs. Kids feel desperate at our age and they feel they have no options sometimes except to hurt themselves. Or when all options are closed, parents don't seem to care, friends don't seem to be there, and other supports just aren't available.

These passages are the raw reality, scribbled in blood by these kids who have found a way to write the words they dare not say aloud to parents or other adults, except perhaps to strangers.

This idea of writing as therapeutic is important and, in fact, could be used as a "reversal technique" to help teenagers deal with their feelings and/or suicidal ideations. I think the teenage narratives revealed in these notes are really the most significant aspect of this book and provide stark insight into a range of issues affecting teenagers.

Today, kid culture coalesces around an intermixture of styles, belief systems, fashion, music, and drugs. It's a new age. Technology is fast and furious. The Internet is often incomprehensible, or at least confusing, to most parents, but because of the technology, our kids are faster too. They're growing up faster, though I am not sure what growing up means anymore. Because of this speed aesthetic, the generation of kids raised in the 1990s is pointing to a "revolution"—in values, morality, and ideals. And the manifestations we see—suicide, drugs, sex, clothing, and music genres—are the ways they experience and communicate their dissatisfaction with the status quo. Megan told me:

The reasons you have so many kids doing sex is because kids have access to sex worlds adults can't touch, can't prohibit, and can't censor like they used to. Parents can't control Internet access or videos, not even television and movies, because they don't have the time anymore. There is no way a parent can control every hour of a teenager's day.

These are signs not of changes to come but of changes already here. Answers to the teen question "Who am I and where do I fit?" are being expressed through behavior that adults, and society at large, can't quite fathom. Boots, with his usual insight, said, "We can have shows about vampires, but not about real kids doing vampirish stuff. As soon as you put on a black trench coat, people label you as different, as you actually are."

I believe teens' high suicide rates represent a rupture, a fissure, a moral fault line, a crack in the foundation of our society. Though likening it to an earthquake might initially seem extreme, it may well be more apt than it would appear. And the possibility that we could have as many as sixty million confused, resentful, bored teenagers means that we could be facing another period like the 1960s, when a revolution occurred that affected everything from sex to politics.

America's kids are killing themselves in unprecedented numbers because they refuse to refrain from expressing real rage and are no longer willing to maintain the tremendous discipline it would take to do so. But this might point to an individual rather than a societal problem. Teens are supposed to live the good life that their parents have provided for them, not kill themselves. The irony—which is totally logical, in light of the commercial exploitation of the teenage body—is that teenagers have found a way to express their rage against family, against indifference, and against society by hurting and/or killing themselves. Suicide is the ultimate act of self-directed rebellion. Because teens—and white teens, in particular—feel guilt about betraying family, community, and country, they are willing to make that level of sacrifice to get us to listen.

Parents must pay attention to this appalling form of warning and not simply turn their backs and walk away, which is how every child feels when we don't see the signs right before our eyes, because it is we who are cowardly and acting out in the eyes of our kids as irresponsible and weak. We need to listen to our kids and make the changes they need in order to heal and to feel whole and purposeful. Throughout this book, the kids have made it clear that many would rather die than deal with this life, this culture, this society. It seems that, because American society has robbed them of their dignity, has destroyed their feelings, they feel death is a peaceful way out. These kids are making a statement with these suicides and suicide attempts. What is a more drastic protest than dying? These kids want to have the final say in what happens to them. They want to have a voice, and death is becoming that voice, screaming out their final words.

EPILOGUE

- **Kyra** still lives at home with her mother. She attends school, taking theater and film studies.
- **Enoch** works in a small town but prefers not to say where.
- **Candy**'s story is like that of a ghost, a kind of legacy narrative written by Megan, as if she were still here with us.
- **Lorrie**, who provided a narrative about **David**, continued to attend college and moved back to California after graduation.
- **Tucker** says the suicide of two friends was a cathartic moment; however, he still struggles with personal issues.
- **Gita**'s whereabouts are unknown.
- **Boots** attended college and lives in New York City.
- **Jill** moved to a small town west of Los Angeles after graduating from high school.
- **Cody** got a job as a blacksmith's apprentice.
- **Gabriella**'s whereabouts are unknown.
- **Megan** moved to New Orleans, and we talked briefly about her wanting to interview street people.

ACKNOWLEDGMENTS

During the early years of this book's development, a number of people were kind enough to assist me. First among them was Dr. Lucille Perez, who was at that time associate director of the Center for Substance Abuse Prevention (CSAP), a branch of Substance Abuse and Mental Health Services Administration (SAMHSA). Dr. Perez was extremely gracious and unselfish in her time and support. Dr. Susan Kornblum provided wonderful insight into the world of teen depression and offered scintillating thoughts concerning adolescent psychology. Thanks also to colleagues Dr. Howard Steele, who gave valuable critique and suggestions concerning the book; and Dean Will Milberg, whose consistent support is especially appreciated. Bettine Josties and Ahad Ali's fine writing and theoretical sophistication provided excellent help with the manuscript. Hakim Hasan's brilliant editorial skills helped make the early draft of the work intellectually refreshing. I owe a great debt to my team of graduate students—Rezvaneh Ganji, Mark Flora, Scott Beck, and Conrad Walker—and to all the students who stuck with me during the 2016 Urban Sociology course, along with my able research assistant and amanuensis Dara Levendosky. I also thank Josh Behar and Lydia Wills who initially saw the value in this work and were extremely important in getting it into early publishable form. I sincerely appreciate the assistance of several Princeton students, especially Chloe Haimson, whose notes help me understand the stories of young women on college campuses.

Of all the people who helped to make this book a reality, none deserve appreciation more than Chloe Lee, who was responsible for bringing many of the teenagers whom this book profiles to my attention. Many thanks also to Jacob, Claire, Holly, Leah, Amanda, Nick, Jill, Cody, Tucker, Candy, Enoch, Ryan, and Gita, all of whom assisted in one way or another with their ideas, personal accounts, or introductions to other young people. A heartfelt thank you and a great deal of appreciation to Boots, Kyra, Gabriella, and Lorrie. I appreciate the families of Gabriella, Ryan, and Chloe, as well as other mothers and fathers who allowed me the privilege of interviewing them about their children.

Thanks to Columbia University Press's marvelous staff, including Eric Schwartz, the editorial director; Cathy Felgar; Lowell Frye; and the sensational CUP artist corps, whose graphic design continues to show fine precision craft in artwork. I thank Todd Manza whose hard work and steadfast assistance was extremely helpful. I would also like to thank Errol James, Brina Goldfarb, Tanya Parker, Ale Smith, Ipe Kgositsile, Joan Morgan, Sharon Ellis, Christina Head, Khalil Hicks, and all the other Harlem Writers Crew Project members because they brought insight and élan to the world of teenagers and helped me understand the complex and often secret world these young people inhabit. I thank my sons Neruda and Kahlil Zulu for their knowledge of street kids and art. Thanks also to their friends Issac, Kahlil, Sharon and Joan, Ipeleng, the Jungle Brothers, and Q-Tip, all of whom provided key information even when they thought they weren't. I would like to thank all my students at Lang College and my New School graduate students including Alessandra Seggi, who provided stimulating discussions about teen life and culture in my classes. Dr. Carla Barrett and Dr. Katia Perea were two stalwart assistants who took over the reins of the Harlem Writers Crew during my absence from the New School. The project came to the New School thanks to warm guiding support from then president Jonathan Fanton. I thank the principal and teachers at City-as-School for introducing kids to the project. Corinna Fales and Penelope Franklin edited parts of the manuscript in its infancy; they were a great delight to work with, and I have an enormous appreciation for their timely skills. The board members of the Harlem Writers Crew Project deserve thanks, especially Robert Simels who mentored, gave his valuable time and financial support, and employed the kids and young adults. Thanks also to board members Gina Kolata, Natalia Filippova, Bill Kornblum, Jonathan Fanton, Jeff Goldfarb, Lucile Perez, Lydia Wills, Melvina Ellis, and the anonymous New York law firm that provided pro bono assistance in setting up the HWCF 501-(c) 3. Finally, thanks go to all the people who financially sponsored the Crew. Though many helped make this book possible, I take sole responsibility for its shortcomings.

APPENDIX A

Ipe and Brownson

The stories of Ipe and Brownson are complementary in many ways, because both stories represent aspects of rape and sex. I did not have enough information to warrant a fuller examination of the issue in the book, but both cases are important. Ipe was the victim of acquaintance rape; Brownson was raped in prison. A large number of such young victims attempt or commit suicide, and rape of adolescents is a common occurrence both in U.S. prisons and in everyday life. Unfortunately, we have no real numbers or information about the incidents of rape and suicide among teens accosted in prisons, though we do know that it happens. Date rape and other forms of acquaintance rape of young women in schools, on college campuses, and in homes is commonplace, though it now is more openly discussed.[1] In fact, acquaintance rape is much more prevalent than stranger rape. A 1995 study published by the Department of Justice reported that 82 percent of victims were raped by someone they knew.[2]

In Brownson's story, rape represents a form of torture, whereas in Ipe's case, if we use Baudrillard's definition, "genuine rape is not forcibly enjoying someone but forcing someone to have pleasure."[3] For both Ipe and Brownson, this is akin to torture. Jana Leo described it this way:

Even more perverse, rape is to force someone to be part of you. There are two forms of torture in rape: passive torture and active torture. Passive torture is experienced in violent rapes; active torture, in nonviolent rapes. In a violent rape there is a higher degree of raw violence and in a nonviolent rape, a higher degree of coercion.[4]

Although stories about rape are numerous these days in the news, the situation faced by young women like Ipe remains all too common. Her truncated yet poignant story is significant because it describes the world girls and women face every day in schools, colleges, and the street. Ipe was recruited, along with several other teenagers growing up in New York City housing project neighborhoods, to write about her life. These experiences involved the tension between identity and change, which is part of the hard process of coming of age that kids like Ipe and Brownson talk and write about.

In some ways, these two pieces of writing are part of a process of "rendering human" youth who represent two different yet similar kinds of feelings, though neither writer is able to fully express or come to terms with his or her experience or particular life conditions. Ipe attempts to discuss and reflect upon her situation, whereas Brownson is completely blocked from doing so. In many ways, this is part of the dilemma of the text, because as storytellers, they are only telling part of their story. Ipe has learned to be increasingly articulate in describing how she sees her own life, the experience of being a young black woman, and the wider world of culture and politics, whereas Brownson has lived a sheltered, shattered life of drink and pent-up anger at his situation.

As I got to know Ipe, through group meetings and debates, and came to know both her mother and her father tangentially,

I also became aware of the narrative beauty of her story. On the other hand, I knew nothing of Brownson, save what I gleaned from transcripts, a short jailhouse interview, and information I received from his court-appointed legal team. In fact, not even the lawyers knew about the rape Brownson had experienced while in custody, nor did he mention this to the court. In order for the life he lived to be of interest, I needed to have documentation of certain facts, and those facts needed to be checked not only against my own ideas and evaluations but also against those of others, such as psychologists, social workers, or other professionals, who could attest to Brownson's well-being.

In addition, as a writer, my function is to present his story, to reveal the full human account as he would tell it in his own words, reflecting his own attitudes and his own feelings, but such an account was not possible here, due to the brevity of our encounter. I usually draw heavily on self-narratives, gathered through interviews, to capture how an interviewee sees himself in his situation. The work here is supposed to be an extended face-to-face engagement, which involves a relationship that goes beyond what is normally seen as "objective" research, even though, as sociologist Ann Mische told me, "When people tell their own stories, they engage in a process of constructing and reconstructing events and attitudes that involves both themselves and the listener in a process of continuous reevaluation and change."

In this way, when I ask Brownson or others to let me into their world, I usually, at the same time, pull them out of their world and into my own. By doing do, I hope that they may gain a critical distance on their experience that assists them in the process of constructing alternatives. I was not able to bring Brownson into my world, and this made his story one-sided and essentially unfulfilled.

I take a personal approach to doing this work. I have always tried to be true to the spirit of the underground populations I study and to describe the various layers of their social experience in as raw and visceral a form as possible. In addition to detailed field observations, therefore, I draw on self-narratives that my contacts, informants, and sponsors have collected through interviews, journals, and diaries, and much of this did not exist in Brownson's case.

IPE'S NOTE

Thoughts

I was repeatedly raped by "the boy next door" my freshman year of high school. That was eight years ago. Male violence against women is as American as apple pie. Television and movie screens reek of sexual violence. Women in print are used to satisfy male consumerism. Rap music has given birth to all sorts of bitches and ho's. Yet I dig Ice-Cube. Cool G Rap. LL Cool J. Brand Nubians. Lord Finnesse. Slick Rick . . . I am a victim of this society's sexist mentality. Yet I am also disgusted with, and scared by, the fact that there is a very fine line dividing those who tell sexist jokes and those who follow through with violent crimes against women.

One

The D's. Dad and divorce leads me searching for a piece of dad from boys and men who are basically dicks. But then there are the uncles. All of Papa's ace boon coons who love and look out since there is no dad in New York City. I make Papa by taking a little piece of everyone and making them into one collective dad. Smile. It is now time get to know my Main Man since his ever present love vanished after the divorce making me terribly insecure and very angry with him today. Peace.

Two

In elementary school I was known for my jean skirt with Kimberly diamonds sewn in by my mother. I was known for consistently winning Spelling Bees. Playing the lead role in any number of plays. Having a high reading score. Enjoying my dance classes. Being a great dancer. I was known for my amiable personality, intelligence and big butt. This was in Harlem.

In Dalton's ruling class environment I had neither dreams nor goals. Simply wishes. Sued Pumas or maybe it was Filas. Lees. Gold shrimp or bamboo earrings. That's because I grew up above 125th on the West Side of Manhattan. I also wished for Tretorns or K-Swiss sneakers, GUESS? jeans and Benetton sweaters. I wished for my best friend's fair red skin and auburn hair. I wished for her relaxer instead of my recently cut short AFRO. And I was terribly eager to have a boyfriend.

The Schmuck lived on my floor in the building where I grew up. It's a very simple story. There's no need for any graphic details. I am simply sharing because at thirteen I would not have felt as alone if I knew how often women are raped in America. He knew and knows my mother hates him. Like smoking cigarettes and experimenting with herb and alcohol it was an act of rebellion. Girls with good sense knew he was trash. Any girl with good sense would not spend their only time with their "boyfriend" who was a pothead and addicted to cocaine smooching in the hallways of her building. I was insecure and therefore attracted to him. It's difficult to admit however it's the truth.

He'd always appear in the hallway after hearing our door close or when I was leaving a girlfriend's apartment. Heavy petting in the hallway continued through the summer. The week before ninth Grade I went shopping. In his brite orange T. Shirt, Jeans and Adidas he saw me from his window, waited by the elevator on our floor, dragged me to his apartment and attempted to rape me. I began closing my door quietly and using the building's staircases rather than riding the elevator. My method was not successful the night before my fourteenth birthday. He claimed he would tell my mother if I did not submit to his sexual needs. I believed him. The summer after the school year my soul was cleansed by spending three months with my father in Africa. When I returned to New York City I stopped speaking to him. The second day of tenth grade he stooped to dragging me down the hallway as a retarded neighbor spotted him.

On my seventeenth birthday I told my mother about the rape. Mother let me know there is no way she could be angry with me which found supportive and loving. It's affected me negatively for every year I let pass without dealing with the fact that a violent crime was committed against me and I don't want the normality of rape to continue.

Three

I was so lacking in self confidence that no boys liked me in high school. Junior Year. One of my classmates was killed by a Mack truck in the South Bronx during the spring. I expressed my anger getting drunk to the point where I was sick at any Dalton party. At the end of the school year one of Dalton's finest boys asked me to the prom. IT spread around the school like that afternoon like no other piece of gossip since he's white and I'm black. I got sick at the prom. Senior year of high school I knew I had to go to an all women's college since I'd been stripped of my self confidence between the divorce, Dalton and Rape.

Four

I spent first semester with my father and joined my all women's feminist academic institution in the boonies of Pennsylvania for the next year and a half. I left being disgusted with the realization that I was at an Ivory Tower. I could not deal with a library that only catered to everything that is Western and European WHITE! I got sick of white women's version of feminism and the concept of being "politically correct." People should be defined by actions not theories however it appeared that the most dominant voice on campus (white radical lesbian feminist students) judged others according to their minds. This bothered me as the students' world did not extend past the college to the community where the campus was located.

Five

New York. Cotton-Lycra. And why is it that we (women) dress half naked? Cotton-Lycra cannot be worn by a woman above fourteenth street otherwise she will be sexually harassed in the streets. The day I wore cotton-Lycra on the train men undressed me with their eyes.

I'm wearing jeans and Mickey Mouse T-shirt when some man asks were the #6 train is. I don't know. So he glares at me and says, "come here woman!" I say, "FUCK YOU!"

A friend is visiting from out of town and decides to find safety riding a bus or subway to walking since everyman is hissing or saying, "Mira-Mira! or "come here baby!"

This behavior is not limited to the streets. I'm the only female in an office filled with young men. Someone plays a song by Eazy E of NWA telling some girl how to suck his dick. Someone asks if I learned anything.

The Jungle Brothers performance of their song "Black Woman" appears quite phony. However, I wish the nappy headed creatures of the Native Tongues Posse had Given birth to the New School of Afrocentric and Culturally Aware Rappers in 1983 so I could have been as proud and comfortable with my person as I am now.

I am angry that Euzene Phalcy is never mentioned amongst Spike Lee, Keenan Wayans or Robert Townsend when discussing young black filmmakers.

UNDERTAKER

Brownson, an eighteen-year-old black male who was raped in prison, writes:

> What you are about to read is the last time you will ever hear from me. This is some serious shit. Whatever you do don't let the second part of this letter end up in the wrong person hands.

Although some teenagers think about killing themselves, they also think about killing others—family members, other kids, or strangers who have harassed them, bullied them, or treated them unfairly. Brownson is a young man who was accused and later convicted of a gruesome crime. One December night, Brownson and two friends had gone on a drinking binge, consuming a half bottle of gin and several joints of marijuana. He stopped at a friend's house, borrowed a gun, drove to a local game room, and commenced firing, killing four people and wounding one, who was paralyzed. He then went to another location a few hours later and killed another man.

Once Brownson was locked in his cell, he wrote what appeared to be a letter camouflaged as nonsensical scribbling but which turned out to be a suicide note to a girlfriend.[5] In the course of writing this book, I encountered a number of teen suicide stories that came with an unclear note or a confusing diary or journal. In some cases, there was no note at all. In Brownson's case, there was a note, but it was indecipherable at first.

At the time of our interview, Brownson was an unhappy-looking kid, about five feet nine, 135 pounds. His short-cut hair covers more of his head than usual, much as a cap would, with the temples and top of his hair running over, giving him a kind of horseshoe hairline. His eyebrows meet in the middle of his face, touching slightly, and in spite of a slight, wan smile, he has a somber look. His eyes are expressive, but his gaze is downcast and to the side. A small scar on his left arm and twin scratches on his forehead look recent. His hands are short, the fingers stubby. His fingernails are bitten down, with the exception of the left pinky nail, which is long and pointed.

Brownson sat in a holding pen at the local courthouse in North Carolina, pensive and unassuming. On the wall behind his eight-by-twelve-foot holding cell was scrawled a Folks gang graffito in the shape of a swastika. I talked to him as a guard stood by. I had become involved in his case as an expert witness, called to testify for the defense about his possible involvement as a gang member, based solely on information contained in letters he'd written to his girlfriend.

My talk with Brownson was privileged and no taping was allowed in his holding cell. On January 2, 1995, Brownson was charged with five counts of first-degree murder and one count of assault with a deadly weapon with intent to kill.

Decoded, one of Brownson's letters to his girlfriend read, in part:

Nikki:

Once again I'm here to drop the fucking bomb on your piece, so you can see for yourself and let niggas know that I can't be fucked with. The shit Im about to tell you is some real shit, it may not seem that way to you, but that shit is real to be believe that!!

First of all I would like to say if you really understood me then you would know why I chosed undertaker to be my new name and if I ever get the intention that you're getting to know me or better yet understand me I will change up my style cause Im not to be understood by anybody. And Im not trying to be smart either. Im a nigga up on you without you knowing, so don't try and get a understanding of me cause I must & will lose you in the process.

This letter was signed "undertaker" and had the numbers 720 525 and *7-4-14, which the authorities took to have gang significance, and this was the main reason Brownson was believed to be gang affiliated. Though the numbers did hold symbolic gang meaning, however, Brownson was not a gang member.[6]

As an ethnographer, I have occasionally appeared in court as an expert witness on matters related to gangs, gang symbols, gang behavior, and decoding street language. In this case, the prosecution argued that Brownson was either into devil worship, the Goth scene, the occult, or gang initiation, and that was why he had committed the murders. I was permitted to interview him, to read his letters, and to examine his confession as well as all statements made by witnesses to the crime. I was asked to determine, based on the interview, the letters (written in gang alphabetical coded letter script) and the state's translations, and handwriting samples, to determine whether any of those theories were true. I also had the chance to review other court-related evidentiary items, such as the postmarked letters with key dates and the alphabet code used in those letters. None of the evidence showed Brownson to be a gang member or a member of the occult, into the Goth scene or devil worship. So why did he kill? We may never know.

Since I was not convinced Brownson was part of any gang or crew, I thought he might be a fake or "wannabe" gang member. It is impossible to be a member of the Crips, Bloods, Vice Lords, or Folks without undergoing initiation rites, including body modification marks (tattoos) to indicate membership, but Brownson had no such tattoos. In addition, gang members require single-group loyalty, and Brownson did not exhibit such loyalty; he used several types of gang symbols in the letters he wrote. I believe he was inconsistent with the symbolism because he did not understand the symbolic meaning of what he was writing and only wanted to impress others on the outside, most likely his girlfriend.

I did have theories about why Brownson tried to commit suicide, but even that is not conclusive.

One way to write a suicide note is to scribble a last will and testament on a piece of paper, or in a diary, or in a journal, describing why one wishes to end life. Instead of writing a note, some teenagers phone a friend, a family member, or even a stranger, such as calls to suicide help lines or the police, indicating suicidal intentions.

My journal notes on my meeting with Brownson read:

September 1996
North Carolina Court House
 A guard stood outside and I was let into his cell. I was a bit nervous and I guess it showed. To be in a cage is an odd strange feeling. I knew I would be getting out in short order but what if you're there for years as surely this man/child will be. There is nothing tough looking about the kid. He's 18 year old —— Brownson about 5-9 or so, skinny, with a querulous voice. He has a baby face, with no facial hair or mustache or sign of one. His hair is cut short and a slight wrinkle comes into his forehead as he squint his nose when he looks up. He doesn't look so much at me but kind of side glances my way. I sit down in a chair provided by the guard. It is hard for me to imagine him fitting the charges of which he's accused. The circumstances of my visit was based on my appearing as an expert witness in his trial for the defense who wanted me to interview him in order to determine a number of factors. One, was he a gang member and two, could he help illuminate the strange scribblings in his letters to his girlfriend. I had already made certain assumptions about the lettering and decoded it sure enough but I wanted to know what the numbers meant and why did he write this in the first place. The interview did not last long, but he was extremely shy and I found myself

feeling sorry for him and wondering how am I going to get this kid to talk to me about himself with a guard outside and me; a person he has never seen before in 12 x 12 foot holding pen. I introduced myself and told him I was there at the request of his court appointed lawyer, Mr ——. He shook his head (affirmatively) and said he knew him. I thought it was an odd response. But after a few minutes of silence he ask if I was a lawyer too. I explained what I did professionally, the ethnographer bit, and cut it short when I realized he was not interested and switched to tell him some of the things I had done with kids in New York and when I said that he said surprisingly, "Have any of them been raped?" I explained one of the girls I was writing about had been but then he said, "No, I mean boys." At this point he began to tell me about what happened to him. This was surely an unusual turn of event situation and certainly not based on any particular skills that I have but just a situation where the young boy decided at that moment to say what had happened to him, perhaps he felt I might convey sympathy for him with the court, I don't know. All I know is at that one point, this shy kid decided to tell me what had happened to him and ironically he said nothing about the murders and seemed as if he was totally detached from that reality which brought him to be in that cell, that day accused of killing five human beings. Two weeks before my visit, Brownson had attempted suicide. His suicidal gesture came about, he told me, after he was raped, and after his girlfriend had decided to stop visiting him because the police had visited her home, questioning her about the murders. He told me about the rape and the suicide attempt:

> They had taken my laces, my belt, and put me in the back cell. Every time I went to the bathroom, I'd bleed. I hated them

motherfuckers, but one was so big, about three hundred pounds, I think, and he held me down at first, but about six of them actually fucked with me. Every time I tried to move, one of them kept a knife to my throat. Then I saw the guards looking at me, and they did nothing until about half an hour later, and so I knew they were in on the whole thing.

I decided to take the shirt I had and wet it and wring it until it fit around my neck. I strung it around my cell bar, but then from the end of the bed it came loose and I hit my head. The next thing I knew, I was on a stretcher, and one of the guards was saying I was stupid to do what I did.

Brownson's comment about the guards observing and doing nothing was a poignant moment in his experience. Brownson has already been quite damaged by his parents—no one is listening to him and nothing is helping. Then he ends up in jail, and the only parental figures left in his life (the guards) not only don't care enough to act responsibly when he gets raped but actually stand idly by and watch.

I wanted to see whether he had written other letters, and to examine those letters to determine whether they held any clue about his being a gang member. But when I asked him what he had said to the police, he said he had confessed to the crime. I later got a copy of his confession report, which stated:

I shot them, I shot them all. I went to the game room with my brother Benny and another kid Taft —— and we shot pool, and I had been drinking before I went there. I had drank about half gallon of Gilbert's Gin. I had also smoked about three joints. It was after dark and we were there for about thirty to forty minutes. I had on some black pants and a red shirt and my sneakers. We left and went to my brother's house who lives in Jasonville lane where

I asked my friend Shawn if he would let me borrow his nine mil-
limeter pistol. He gave it to me and I told him I was going back
to the pool hall and kill everybody in there. But I don't think he
shoulda given me that gun. I was drunk. I was drunk and there
was no telling what was going through my head. Anyway another
friend, Michael ———, asked me if I was ready and he drove me to
the game room where he parked the truck on the south side of
the road and walked over to the game room. I walked in and as
far as I know Michael stood outside. I walked to the small window and shot in and shot the fat guy. He was the first one I shot.
I then walked to the back and shot Billy and the other boy and
they both dropped and at first I did not know which one I had hit
first until I saw Billy crawling under the pool table and I figured
I had hit the white boy. I slide back on the pistol and a bullet fell
out and then I shot underneath the pool table and I did not know
if I had hit him or not and he ran out of the game room and I did
not see Michael anywhere near the door. I ran after Billy and I
fired twice, until the clip ran out of bullet. I then ran outside and I
saw Michael across the road running towards the truck and I saw
Billy running across the field to my right. I then ran and caught
up with Michael and we got into the truck and Michael asked me
what had happened and I told him that I shot all of them and that
was that.

The three teenagers mentioned at the scene were arrested by
the police and gave statements regarding the murders, some of
which contradicted Brownson's testimony.

The sixth person shot, and the fifth to die, was shot before
midnight at another location. According to eyewitness Michael:

On Saturday night about 11:30 PM I was at 200 Double View
lane visiting my brother and I had left with Ben and his brother

Rod. Ben was driving a blue Toyota pickup truck: dark blue and Rod wanted us to drop him off at the Game Room on Crabtree Road. And Rod said that he had been there earlier and that he needed to go back to get some weed meaning marijuana. He said to drop him off and come back and get him in five minutes. We dropped him off at the road and turned and drive to the 801 housing area and drove through and drive back and Rod was standing on the side of Tivoli Road and we stopped and picked him up and were driving west on Tivoli Road when Rod said, "I shot all five of them." Ben then said, "Why did you do something like that man?" Rod then said if we told anyone that we would get the same thing. Rod acted like he didn't care about what he said he had just done. That it didn't bother him. Rod then told us to drive to Harmony Heights because he had heard that there was a party going on over there. He had on black jeans, a red shirt and a black jacket. [This part of the confession sounds like he's being prompted to add details.] He had on black toboggan cap. After we went to Harmony heights and there was no party going on, we went back to Ben's house and then we left and drove the blue truck and Rod was with me and we went to the Zodiac club on Vass Road.

It was there and I saw Ben and Aaron —— arguing. I do not know what they were arguing about and James —— walked up between them and tried to get them to stop arguing and Rod walked up and stuck a black pistol up to the side James head and pulled the trigger and shot him.

Psychologist Ronald W. Maris examined young blacks in the Chicago area who had conflicts with the police and other institutional authorities, and he concluded that the black suicides he examined were the result of retroflex anger (anger turned inward) rather than of depression.[7] To many psychologists, this is the definition of depression today. Maris interpreted these suicides as reactions to social crises—ending a relationship with a girlfriend or spouse, for example, or being arrested and spending time in jail. Brownson's suicide attempt seems mostly related to his sexual humiliation in prison and to the death of five people he now has to serve the rest of his life thinking about.

Much controversy surrounds the connection between imprisonment and suicide, and the link is increasingly fodder for conspiracy theorists. It may be that fear of the police and feelings of powerlessness in dealing with all-white authority are critical to explaining jail-related black teen suicide and suicide attempts.

In some ways, ethnographers are less interested in unique individuals than in explaining the behavior of groups of people and how the behavior of the individual is influenced by membership in social groups. I believe kids and young people, especially, are most satisfied with their lives when their day-to-day behavior is oriented (at least in part) toward a set of meaningful goals and is regulated by a set of norms and rules. When these goals lose their meaning, the individual becomes less interested in what life has to offer, and the possibility of suicide increases. I believe, as Émile Durkheim reasoned, that any quick or rapid change in society as a whole, or in an individual's life or social situation, will create rootlessness, or what he called "anomie," and will increase the probability of suicide.[8]

Today, Ipe lives in California and is attending university. Brownson is serving a life sentence somewhere in the United States.

APPENDIX B

Enoch and His Brother

I asked Enoch to recap his life and to describe what has been going on with him over the past few years, noting that our last conversation was in the summer of 2001. About that time, he said,

> I was in a transition period and heavily invested in religion and this negative identity. I was taking lots of drugs, too. I probably didn't tell you all about that then, did I?

He laughs quickly, to indicate he's had a few tabs of LSD, mushrooms, and such.

> I was taking about fifty tabs [of LSD] a week, and I went to see Cody in New Orleans. I was hitching and hopping trains at that time and it was fun but not something that made me feel very good about myself. I gave away all my stuff—my car, a bunch of stuff—and I only kept enough to fit into a backpack, and ended up in Pittsburgh, where I lived in some squats, then moved on to Minneapolis. You see, I never really felt part of any group thing.

CHILDHOOD

You gotta remember, all through my childhood, from kindergarten on through, I was in therapy. At about the time I was seeing Cody down there [in New Orleans], my little brother was in second grade and I was on my way out of our town and my dad was going on those weekenders, those benders—alcohol benders—because he would be gone for days at a time.

But I was always taking my little brother with me to school. I was very protective of him and I didn't want my father to be with him. I would call my little brother my son, not my little brother, so I could protect him. I felt he would be better-rounded human being than I was if I could protect him.

But I left home when I was fifteen and came back at seventeen—that was around 2003. That was when I went off to hop on those trains again and ended up on Saratoga, near the racetrack. And I had developed that Bosnian accent and started doing fortune-telling and got people to pay me and started making money doing fortunes. Then I went to Pittsburgh for a while.

THE SUMAC TREE

I got my ass touched by a poison sumac tree and coulda died, because if you don't treat that right away you could be in trouble, if you don't take care of that. [Brushing up against sumac leaves or berries releases urushiol, which causes a rash.]

But I wanted to get back to that town ———, because I didn't want my father to develop any kind of relationship with my little brother, Samuel. He was eleven years old and we started to get even closer at that time and we could get together more and more. And by the time he turned fifteen and sixteen he started also to get drunk on occasion, and my approach was to do, *Okay, I'll get drunk with him but do it responsibly and that will make him do it responsibly too.* But I guess that didn't work out too well, because I was not doing it responsibly enough, since I started drinking more. This was a bad idea. But at seventeen he was doing better and got a job working with me painting houses, and over the winter there wasn't much to do. And he had come back to —— and he went out with a bunch of his friends and brought everybody some food and booze, got involved with some altercation at the local gas station, and the cashier there called the police.

He was already full of alcohol, so the cops arrested him and found out he was underage, and they threatened to send him to juvie [juvenile detention] and they brought him to my mother's house. The cops told him he had four strikes against him, because he had been arrested a couple times before for drinking, and that he would have to go jail this time. It was four in the morning and he locked himself in his room.

Well, we live in a gun culture around here and he had a gun in his room. He was being rebellious anyway, and while we were downstairs we heard this loud sound and it sounded like a gun going off. I heard the gun go off but I didn't think it was his gun. You know, you hear and see these things on TV. When you do hear them, you think they happen to everybody else but you.

So. I left and then came back and went over to his house, as things had quieted down by then, and the whole thing is such a bizarre thing, but it was a real shocker, as the police were there and they had taken his body away and they didn't have nobody to clean up the room. The medics don't do it, the cops don't do it, the ambulance people don't do it, and certainly my mom couldn't do it. Nobody gives you a box of bleach and tissues to do it, so I had to do it.

Enoch's voice broke off.

Over the next few days, I went over there and had to take the blood off the walls, pick the hair out of the wall, bits of skull out of the walls. I spent months thinking about this whole scenario—what happened before that situation happened, seeing his face, reliving what we did that day, and just thinking I would see him walking down the street. I would turn the corner and expect to see him bumping into me or see him standing where I used to see him.

After Enoch went to the house to clean up his brother's remains, he could not stop thinking about what had happened. The whole thing was too surreal.

I would carry a piece of his skull in my pocket, just to remind myself of him, as a way to make me think of him. That whole episode shut me down for a long time. This was a tough time for me to get close to people, and I started drinking hard—real hard—and of course I drove a lot of people away from me. I wanted to join the military because I thought that would help me get some structure, and just as a way to deal with life.

This was up to 2012 or so. I would be drinking from morning to night. I would get up in the morning and drink and go to bed with a bottle in my hand. I would think about Samuel and, believe it or not, I found myself getting angry at him for killing himself, angry at him for dying on me, because I resented him for leaving me. And of course I began to think of suicide myself. I kept a gun in my room and would put it on my lap. Many times did I think about the situation and how it would play out. Then I would calm down and say to myself not to do this. So many times I would be alone and I just could not stop thinking about killing myself. You see, I would have a gun next to me and I would sit there with the gun on my lap. I had become a butcher at that time, and I had a knife at my throat and thought about cutting my own throat.

Enoch said so much was happening in his head, thoughts rushed in and out, and life became a blur.

Finally, one day my girlfriend left me and I started with the co-caine. That was back in 2013, about four years ago, and that was when I was no longer a teenager, no longer a young man, but I was not thirty, and that was when she left me. At thirty was a tough time, a tough year, because that was when everybody, all my friends my age, started to see the dreams faded, because it was then you could see whether you were going to be somebody or not—that was the year. If you were single, [if] you had the house and the kids and the boring dead-end jobs or not, and that was going to be it for the rest of your life. You were not going anywhere now, at thirty. All my friends were settled, and if you had any dreams, they were now gone, and if you hadn't done it by thirty you were not going to do it. This was the year people gave up on themselves. There was no promising future after thirty. After my thirty birthday, I was starting to block shit out. I was a painter of houses, a bartender, and a butcher.

On that day, my friend Cody called me to say he was bummed out, too, and I told him I needed some support as well, so he and I started drinking for a while. I was miserable. Thinking about my brother's death; couldn't shut it out of my mind. I couldn't shut it out anymore. So I drank some more, but nothing could block it out, so I drank some more. I was thinking about suicide every day. I couldn't look at a knife without thinking about cutting my own body. I had my buddies come by and they had a condo and brought over some strippers and booze but it wasn't any good. I mean, all of this did not make me feel any better, so I just stopped everything. I stopped drinking. I stopped drugging. I stopped doing coke. I just stopped everything altogether.

I don't have thoughts of killing myself, but I sit over this river and I imagine what it would be like to float down the river and sink slowly under. And as I think about how this . . . this imagining helps me, to calm me, and I think what people look like when they are feeling that release and no longer under the pressure and the world is not an uncomfortable place. And, I think, when the world is not an uncomfortable place and I begin imagining the release, then I get this calming, and somehow that calming is the most therapeutic feeling I ever get.

NOTES

PROLOGUE

1. Donna Gaines, *Teenage Wasteland* (Chicago: University of Chicago Press, 1990), 249.

INTRODUCTION

1. Terry Williams, *The Cocaine Kids: The Inside Story of a Teenage Drug Ring* (New York: Da Capo, 1989).
2. Terry Williams, *Crackhouse: Notes from the End of the Line* (New York: Addison-Wesley, 1992).
3. Terry Williams and William Kornblum, *The Uptown Kids: Struggle and Hope in the Projects* (New York: Putnam, 1994); and Jonathan Stack, Terry Williams, and Susanne Szabo Rostock, *Harlem Diary: Nine Voices of Resilience*, documentary film, directed by Jonathan Stack (Discovery Channel in association with Gabriel Films, 1995).
4. Antoon Leenaars, *Suicide Notes: Predictive Clues and Patterns* (New York: Human Sciences Press, 1988), 26.
5. Émile Durkheim, *Suicide: A Study in Sociology* (London: Routledge and Kegan, 1952).
6. Joseph Bensman and Robert Lillienfeld, *Between Public and Private: The Lost Boundaries of the Self* (New York: The Free Press, 1979), 19–25.
7. Loïc Wacquant, *Body and Soul* (Oxford: Oxford University Press, 2004); and Marcel Mauss, "Techniques of the Body," *Economy and Society* 2, no. 1 (1934).

2. THE FIGHTER: ENOCH

1. Albert Camus, *The Myth of Sisyphus and Other Essays* (New York: Vintage Books, 1955), 3.

2. Ethnographer's journal: "The quotes from Enoch's journal entries and conversations are poignant and raw and offer power to his story, but I am concerned about arriving at an interpretive sociological framework that is based on what Enoch has said—which is basically one-dimensional in this narrative. But, after all, it is Enoch's word. It is his story. His narrative outlines a few key points involving domestic abuse and core suicidal trauma, such as rape and incest." I made the above notes based on Enoch's narrative to get a better sense of the internal logic of his suicide notes. I realize the end of Enoch's section is very abrupt (he seems to come out of suicidal impulses miraculously without any real explanation), but Appendix B provides further insight into his recovery.

3. William Styron, *Darkness Visible: A Memoir of Madness* (New York: Vintage Books, 1990), 5.

3. OVERLOAD: CANDY

1. Borderline personality disorder is a mental health disorder that generates significant emotional instability and carries with it a variety of stressful mental behavioral problems. People who suffer from this condition have a severely distorted self-image and usually feel worthless. At the same time, many get better without seeking help or medication. Post-traumatic stress disorder is a condition of persistent mental and emotional stress occurring as a result of injury or severe psychological shock. It typically involves sleep disturbances and constant, vivid recall of the experience, which dulls one's responses to others and to the outside world. I make note of the difference between the current definition of borderline personality disorder, according to the *Diagnostic and Statistical Manual of Mental Disorders*, and post-traumatic stress disorder because I think the relation of these two maladies to suicide or parasuicide is important. See American Psychiatric Association, *Diagnostic*

and Statistical Manual of Mental Disorders, 5th ed. (Washington, DC: American Psychiatric Association, 2013).

4. THE LAST STAND: DAVID

1. Elijah Anderson, *Code of the Street* (New York: W. W. Norton, 1999).

7. SHOCK JOCK: BOOTS

1. Walter J. Torres and Raymond M. Bergner, "Humiliation: Its Nature and Consequences," *Journal of the American Academy of Psychiatry and the Law* 38, no. 2: 195.
2. See Armando Favazza, *Bodies Under Siege: Self-Mutilation, Nonsuicidal Self-Injury, and Body Modification in Culture and Psychiatry* (Baltimore: Johns Hopkins University Press, 1986).
3. bell hooks, *Yearning: Race, Gender, and Cultural Politics* (Cambridge, MA: South End Press, 1990).

8. CUTTER: JILL

1. See Katherine Brady, *Father's Days: A True Story of Incest* (New York: Seaview Books, 1979).
2. See Geo Stone, *Suicide and Attempted Suicide: Methods and Consequences* (New York: Carroll and Graf, 2001).

10. BORN-AGAIN VIRGIN: GABRIELLA

1. Terry Williams, *Harlem Supers: The Social Life of a Community in Transition* (New York: Palgrave Macmillan, 2016).

AFTERWORD

1. Centers for Disease Control and Prevention (CDC), "Injury Prevention and Control: Data and Statistics (WISQARS)," accessed June 11, 2016, http://www.cdc.gov/injury/wisqars/.

2. National Vital Statistics Report, *Morbidity and Mortality Weekly Report.* This report presents detailed data from 1999–2014, including the number of U.S. suicide injury deaths and rates per 100,000 people age thirteen to nineteen, all races, both sexes.

3. Danice K. Eaton et al., "Youth Risk Behavior Surveillance—United States, 2011," *Surveillance Summaries* 61, no 4: 1–162, http://www.cdc.gov/mmwr/preview/mmwrhtml/ss6104a1.htm; and CDC, "Injury Prevention and Control."

4. Jack P. Gibbs, *Suicide: A Sociological Study* (New York: Harper & Row, 1968).

5. Victor Turner, *The Forest of Symbols: Aspects of Ndembu Ritual* (Ithaca, NY: Cornell University Press, 1967), 8.

6. According to the U.S. Census Bureau, in 2008 there were 21,469,780 teenagers age fifteen to nineteen in the United States.

7. Gary Cross, *An All-Consuming Century* (New York: Columbia University Press, 2000).

8. Donna Gaines, *Teenage Wasteland* (Chicago: University of Chicago Press, 1990).

9. David Lester and Calvin Reeve, "The Suicide Notes of Young and Old People," *Psychological Reports* 50, no. 1 (February 1982): 334. See also Stuart Cohen and Joanne Fiedler, "Content Analysis of Multiple Messages in Suicide Notes," *Suicide and Life-Threatening Behavior* 4, no. 2 (Summer 1974): 75–95.

10. Thomas Hine, *The Rise and Fall of the American Teenager* (New York: HarperCollins, 1999).

APPENDIX A. IPE AND BROWNSON

1. See *Rape in America: A Report to the Nation* (Arlington, VA: National Victim Center, 1992); and *Prevalence, Incidence and Consequences of Violence Against Women Survey* (Washington, DC: National Institute of Justice and U.S. Centers for Disease Control and Prevention, 1998). In the second study, researchers interviewed 8,000 women and 8,000 men and used a definition of rape that included forced vaginal, anal, or oral intercourse.

2. Ronet Bachman and Linda Saltzman, *Violence Against Women* (Washington, DC: U.S. Department of Justice, 1995), a Bureau of Justice Statistics Special Report based on data from the National Crime Victimization Survey.

3. Jean Baudrillard, *Impossible Exchange* (New York: Verso Books, 2001), 123.

4. Jana Leo, *Rape New York* (New York: Feminist Press, 2009), 125. Leo makes the case for understanding rape in both violent and nonviolent situations.

5. I should point out that no confidence has been abused in telling this story, and although I have not included all the facts of the case, the account presented is a matter of public record and can be easily verified. This narrative is based on the letters Brownson wrote and on the content of our interview.

6. Numerology is one of the hallmarks of gang culture. The numbers 7, 5, 2, 4, and 0 all have a specific meaning, but numbers often substitute for letters, as well. For example, 274 might be decoded as 2 = *B*, 7 = *G*, and 4 = *D*, which could mean Black Gangsta Disciples. Brownson addresses the letter to "Nikki," which could be code (*N* = nigga, *K* − kill) for "Nigga, I kill, kill, I," or could also be palindromic. The deciphering and interpretation was done by the authorities, and only the Black Gangsta Disciples example rings true to me.

7. Ronald W. Maris, *Social Forces in Urban Suicide* (Homewood, IL: The Dorsey Press, 1969).

8. Émile Durkheim, *Suicide: A Study in Sociology* (London: Routledge and Kegan, 1952).

BIBLIOGRAPHY

Anonymous. *Go Ask Alice.* New York: Simon Pulse, 2006.

Baudrillard, Jean. *Impossible Exchange.* New York: Verso Books, 2001.

Bensman, Joseph, and Robert Lillienfeld. *Between Public and Private: The Lost Boundaries of the Self.* New York: The Free Press, 1979.

Brady, Katherine. *Father's Days: A True Story of Incest.* New York: Seaview Books, 1979.

Cohen, Stuart, and Joanne Fiedler. "Content Analysis of Multiple Messages in Suicide Notes." *Suicide and Life-Threatening Behavior* 4, no. 2 (Summer 1974): 75–95.

Cross, Gary. *An All-Consuming Century.* New York: Columbia University Press, 2000.

Durkheim, Émile. *Suicide: A Study in Sociology.* London: Routledge and Kegan, 1952.

Favazza, Armando. *Bodies Under Siege: Self-Mutilation and Body Modification in Culture and Psychiatry.* Baltimore: Johns Hopkins University Press, 1986.

Gaines, Donna. *Teenage Wasteland: Suburbia's Dead End Kids.* Chicago: University of Chicago Press, 1990.

Ginzberg, Eli, Terry Williams, and Anna Dutka. *Does Job Training Work? The Clients Speak Out.* Boulder, CO: Westview Press, 1991.

Hine, Thomas. *The Rise and Fall of the American Teenager.* New York: Harper Collins, 1999.

hooks, bell. *Yearning: Race, Gender, and Cultural Politics.* Cambridge, MA: South End Press, 1990.

Leenaars, Antoon. *Suicide Notes: Predictive Clues and Patterns.* New York: Human Sciences Press, 1988.

Leo, Jana. *Rape New York.* New York: Feminist Press, 2009.

Lester, David, and Calvin Reeve. "The Suicide Notes of Young and Old People." *Psychological Reports* 50, no. 1 (February 1982), 334.

Maris, Ronald, Alan Berman, and Morton Silverman. *Comprehensive Textbook of Suicidology.* New York: Guilford Press. 2000.

Mauss, Marcel. "Techniques of the Body." *Economy and Society* 2, no. 1 (1934).

Peck, Scott. *The Road Less Traveled: A New Psychology of Love, Traditional Values, and Spiritual Growth.* New York: Touchstone, 1978.

Stack, Jonathan, Terry Williams, and Susanne Szabo Rostock. *Harlem Diary: Nine Voices of Resilience.* Documentary film. Directed by Jonathan Stack. Discovery Channel in association with Gabriel Films, 1995.

Stone, Geo. *Suicide and Attempted Suicide: Methods and Consequences.* New York: Carroll and Graf, 2001.

Styron, William. *Darkness Visible: A Memoir of Madness.* New York: Vintage Books, 1990.

Torres, Walter J., and Raymond M. Bergner, "Humiliation: Its Nature and Consequences." *Journals of American Academy of Psychiatry and the Law* 38, no. 2 (June 2010): 195–204.

Turner, Victor. *The Forest of Symbols: Aspects of Ndembu Ritual.* Ithaca, NY: Cornell University Press, 1967.

Wacquant, Loïc. *Body and Soul.* Oxford: Oxford University Press, 2004.

Williams, Terry. *The Cocaine Kids: The Inside Story of a Teenage Drug Ring.* New York: Da Capo, 1989.

——. *Crackhouse: Notes from the End of the Line.* New York: Addison-Wesley, 1992.

——. *Harlem Supers: The Social Life of a Community in Transition.* New York: Palgrave Macmillan, 2016.

Williams, Terry, and William Kornblum. *Growing Up Poor.* Lanham, MD: Lexington Books, 1985.

——. *The Uptown Kids: Struggle and Hope in the Projects.* New York: Putnam, 1994.

INDEX

248 ❧ Index

Index ❦ 251